Praise P9-CJM-574

"Lofgren's ideas are trenchant and far-reaching. . . . He writes about how the Republican party took advantage of a profoundly ignorant electorate, an easily conned and distracted media, and a cowed Democratic Party to press the ideological struggle in spite of the deep unpopularity of many of its positions."

—George Packer, *The New Yorker*

"A fast-moving, hard-hitting, drily witty account of the radicalization of the Republican party, the failures of Democratic rivals, and the appalling consequences for the country at large. Like the essay that inspired it, *The Party Is Over* is forceful, convincing, and seductive."

—*The Washington Post*

"An engrossing autopsy of current political reality—where one party looks like a freak show and the other barely registers a pulse."

—*Tampa Bay Times*

"A pen in Lofgren's deft hands, combined with his deep understanding of political history and acid sense of humor, becomes a sharp, deeply penetrating harpoon aimed at the heart of his subject. In addition to harpooning the bloated degenerate Republican whale, Mike harpoons the Democrats by demonstrating subtly, yet persuasively, how their growing 'uselessness' arose out of an enervating sense of entitlement to power."

—*Counterpunch*

"A Republican-eye view of what went wrong, beginning with Newt Gingrich's takeover of the Republican Party . . . Lofgren advances our understanding of middle-class issues significantly."

—*Business Insider*

"Lofgren's description of the ins and outs of lawmaking is trenchant and insightful."

—*History Wire*

"A scrupulously bipartisan diagnosis of the sick state of American politics and governance . . . Lofgren devotes close attention to budget issues rarely accorded so much detail in garden-variety op-ed warfare. . . . He has crafted an angry but clear-sighted argument that may not sit well at family reunions or dinner parties, but deserves attention."

—*Publishers Weekly*

"Expect demand for this inside view of Washington, D.C., by a staffer who spent a quarter-century on Capitol Hill . . . Lofgren criticizes Democrats, but his long service to GOP office-holders inevitably makes his critique of that party more detailed and fascinating. . . . A pungent, penetrating insider polemic."

—*Booklist* (starred review)

PENGUIN BOOKS

THE PARTY IS OVER

Mike Lofgren spent twenty-eight years in Congress, the last sixteen as a senior analyst on the House and Senate Budget committees. This gave him a ringside seat on TARP, Hurricane Katrina disaster relief, debates on Pentagon spending, and the inner workings of various deficit-reduction commissions. He holds two degrees in history and received a Fulbright scholarship. He has written for *The Washington Post*, the *Los Angeles Times*, *The Huffington Post*, and *Truthout*, among other publications, and has appeared on *Hardball* and *To the Point*. He lives in Alexandria, Virginia.

THE PARTY

★★★ IS ★★★

OVER

**HOW REPUBLICANS WENT CRAZY,
DEMOCRATS BECAME USELESS,
AND THE MIDDLE CLASS GOT SHAFTED**

Mike Lofgren

PENGUIN BOOKS

PENGUIN BOOKS
Published by the Penguin Group
Penguin Group (USA), 375 Hudson Street,
New York, New York 10014, USA

USA | Canada | UK | Ireland | Australia | New Zealand | India | South Africa | China
Penguin Books Ltd, Registered Offices: 80 Strand, London WC2R 0RL, England
For more information about the Penguin Group visit penguin.com

First published in the United States of America by Viking Penguin,
a member of Penguin Group (USA), 2012
This edition with a new preface published in Penguin Books 2013

Portions of this book appeared in different form as
"Goodbye to All That: Reflections of a GOP Operative Who Left the Cult,"
Truthout, September 3, 2011.

THE LIBRARY OF CONGRESS HAS CATALOGED THE HARDCOVER EDITION
AS FOLLOWS:
Lofgren, Mike.
The party is over : how Republicans went crazy, Democrats became useless,
and the middle class got shafted / Mike Lofgren.
p.   cm.
Includes bibliographical references and index.
ISBN 978-0-670-02626-5 (hc.)
ISBN 978-0-14-312421-4 (pbk.)
1. Republican Party (U.S. : 1854–)—History—20th century. 2. Republican Party
(U.S. : 1854–)—History—21st century. 3. Democratic Party (U.S.)—History—
20th century. 4. Democratic Party (U.S.)—History—21st century.
5. Political parties—United States—History—20th century. 6. Political parties—
United States—History—21st century. I. Title.

Printed in the United States of America
1   3   5   7   9   10   8   6   4   2

Set in Haarlemmer MT Std with Memphis LT Std
Designed by Daniel Lagin

This book is dedicated to the memory of

Earnest Walter Lofgren

Son of working-class Swedish immigrants, child of the Great Depression, honorable veteran of the Pacific campaign, beneficiary of the GI Bill of Rights, and holder of an advanced university degree, for patiently endeavoring to instill in his children his abiding belief in learning

CONTENTS

PREFACE TO THE
PAPERBACK EDITION

As with many religions, political parties have a tendency to start as movements, transform into businesses, and finally degenerate into rackets designed to fleece the yokels. One organization that has embraced this evolution is the Republican Party. And it has done so with a national scope and fundraising apparatus that would have made Jimmy Swaggart or Jim and Tammy Faye Bakker mute with awe.

By "Republican Party" I mean both the formal party and its extended apparat: talk radio and the Fox News empire, pressure groups like the Family Research Council, allegedly "educational" 501(c)3 organizations like the Heritage Foundation, direct-mail outfits descended from the original Richard Viguerie mother ship, polling firms like Rasmussen, and the Tea Party itself, which continues to assert its non-affiliation with the GOP despite having sponsored the Florida Republican presidential candidates' debate in 2011.

True believers in this multifaceted scam are usually careful to make a (false) distinction between the institutional GOP and the so-called conservative movement. The Republican Party and its grandees, according to this fable, are not "true conservatives." By 2008, the operatives of the racket were already saying this about George W. Bush, but that assessment required them to perform the mental gymnastics of forgetting that only a few years earlier they were eager to nominate Dubya to the next available vacancy in the Trinity.

Having abandoned the apostate Bush, they went off on a quixotic hunt for the next messiah: Sarah Palin? Michele Bachmann? The resurrected Newt Gingrich? As each pasteboard messiah eventually fell to earth with a thump, the congregation settled for the colorless but ostensibly electable Mitt Romney, the purest true conservative in the operational sense, given his genius for separating rich donors from their money. That pragmatic decision came to naught in November 2012, but it wasn't long before the faithful, and all the movement's con artists who cling to them like fleas to a dog, were off on a pilgrimage to find the next conservative Wunderkind. Chris Christie, maybe? On second thought, perhaps the temperamental governor lacks the soothing, good-natured bonhomie of Reagan. Marco Rubio, evidently qualified to rebrand the party for a rising demographic because both his names end in vowels? Or maybe even Bobby Jindal? The search for the anointed one continues, much to the amusement of satirists.

It was not always thus. When I came to Washington in the early 1980s, the GOP was the "party of ideas" and seemed on the verge of becoming the dominant political factor on the American scene. The Democrats' venerable New Deal coalition had become stale and was visibly crumbling, while under Reagan, the Republicans offered a "big tent" alternative. After decisively winning the presidency in the 1988 election for the third consecutive term, the GOP was at the height of its national potential. George H. W. Bush had taken California (the last time a Republican presidential candidate did so) and several other states, such as Illinois, Michigan, and New Jersey, that we can now almost always count in the Democratic column. Educated suburban voters, including women, were trending Republican. Soothsayers were declaring that the GOP was on the threshold of political dominance with an "electoral lock."

It was not to be. Triumphs portended overreach. It wasn't long before sane Americans began to regret their electoral decisions. In the 1990s, after winning Congress for the first time in forty years, the GOP proceeded to shut down the government, impeach the chief executive over a bedroom farce, and perform amateur forensic tests to prove that Vince Foster was murdered. Enjoying stratospheric approval ratings (ironically enough in the wake of a national tragedy resulting from his own failure to understand an intelligence briefing), George W. Bush brought us bogus WMDs, the invasion of Iraq, torture, and "heck of a job" Brownie. After retaking the House in 2010, gonzo Republicans promptly marched the country into the first national credit downgrade in our history.

Unchastened by its electoral drubbing in 2012, the GOP circled the wagons once again. Is their former colleague, the war-disabled Bob Dole, pleading with the Senate GOP to ratify a harmless United Nations treaty recommending international standards for the treatment of the disabled? No way, the UN's black helicopters might descend on America! Are hurricane victims still out of their homes in the depth of winter? Screw 'em, they're not our constituents! Is the GOP's filibuster of a nominee for secretary of defense unprecedented? Precedents were made to be broken, and traitors have to be punished! Indeed, freshman Senator Ted Cruz, visually and substantively reprising the role of Joe McCarthy, has even implied treason, slyly insinuating that his former colleague Chuck Hagel might be in the pay of North Korea or Iran. It doesn't end there: the lunatic Right has suggested that John Brennan, the president's CIA Director-designee, and certainly a man involved in killing his share of Muslims, is himself a secret Muslim convert, just like his boss.

Shocking as all this is, it should not be surprising. As the GOP narrowed and hardened its dogma, the affluent, educated suburbs drifted away from the Church of Reagan, leaving the organization to an increasingly less educated, Southern, rural, and downscale white voting base. (The executive wing of the party is decidedly not downscale in its personal finances; they know, just as surely as L. Ron Hubbard knew, that there is gold to be mined from suckers.) The slide among both voters and elected officials has been frighteningly steep since 2008. The current crop of congressional GOP freshmen and sophomores makes George W. Bush look like Henry Cabot Lodge. The party of Abraham Lincoln (a genuine architect of popular enlightenment through his establishment of land-grant colleges) has degenerated into Scientology for rednecks who think, in the words of Congressman Paul Braun (R-GA), that embryology, evolutionary biology, and geology are "lies from the pit of hell."

The deeper causes of this lunacy lie beyond the GOP, for the party is a symptom of a peculiar American sociology. The forty-year-long deindustrialization of the country and the associated weakening of upward mobility for blue-collar Americans are significant factors. Along with deindustrialization came the catastrophic decline of industrial unions, which had once been a secular political outlet for constructive action and social assimilation for workers. The symbiosis of politics and religion in American life, a phenomenon almost unheard of in other advanced democracies these days, infused many politicians with a taste for self-righteousness and apocalyptic brinksmanship that are fatal to a system designed for the separation of powers, compromise, and moderation. Finally, the Cold War lasted too long and left a permanent garrison state; it also left a paranoid worldview that demands enemies foreign and domestic. If the monolithic world Communist conspiracy is no longer with us, the Muslim caliphate will serve nicely in its stead. If there is no longer an internal Red menace boring from within, there is a secret Muslim poised to become CIA director.

☆

What has changed since I wrote the hardcover edition of this book? Following the November 2012 presidential election, media pundits declared the Republican Party finished as a competitive national coalition, or at least in serious jeopardy. Having entered the election season with the Democratic incumbent presiding over an economy suffering from 8 percent unemployment, the GOP deluded itself into thinking it had the presidency in the bag. So much greater was the shock when President Obama coasted to a victory by a margin of nearly five million votes. On Capitol Hill the story was the same: the Democrats picked up two Senate seats in a year when they could have lost their majority. The House remained in Republican hands, but they lost eight seats in their remaining power bastion in Washington.

It was certainly a drubbing, and a few Republican officeholders, like Louisiana governor Bobby Jindal, have insisted the GOP must retool its message and "stop being the stupid party." Even some conservative rabble-rousers like Sean Hannity are now admitting that the party can no longer ignore—let alone disdain—Hispanic voters. Many in the party's base, however, don't want to hear that, or any other plea for pragmatism. Led by increasingly shrill "shock jocks" like Alex Jones, they are fighting to maintain ideological purity. Sensing an intraparty war in the GOP, Democratic pundits are passing the popcorn and radiating self-satisfaction. Have Republicans become so "crazy" (to borrow a word from the subtitle of this book) that they are about to self-destruct?

I would hesitate before pronouncing the Republican Party dead, or even in protracted crisis. It is too well entrenched in too many state legislatures due to gerrymandering. In turn, the state legislatures have gerrymandered congressional districts effectively enough that it is unlikely Republicans will lose control of the House at least until the census of 2020. Dixie and the Tornado Belt will send obstructionists to the Senate for the foreseeable future, thus assuring a veto over legislation via the filibuster. The voting base itself, endlessly stoked by talk radio and Fox News, thrives on its martyrlike self-image as a persecuted remnant of Real Americans. All the would-be messiahs they adore are Republicans, not third-party candidates. And, who knows, another national catastrophe like 9/11 or an asset collapse could once again put them at the helm of the country to summon the demons lurking in the national id.

It is worth reminding those who think the GOP is fading that Republicans actually picked up a gubernatorial seat in 2012 and now control twenty-nine of fifty state governorships. They hold twenty-seven state legislatures, compared to seventeen for the Democrats (the rest have split control). Dominance over state governments—particularly in key states like Ohio, Pennsylvania, Michigan, and Wisconsin—means the GOP will remain a force to be reckoned with for some time, particularly if desperation, opportunism, or zealotry tempts them once again to pervert the instruments of democratic governance to thwart democracy itself.

The GOP's efforts at vote suppression through onerous identification requirements, shortening early voting periods, and changing polling hours did not have the desired effect in 2012. But Republicans in state legislatures have already gone back to the drawing board to concoct new horrors. The Virginia Senate GOP proposed to award the state's electoral votes for president not to the candidate who wins the popular vote statewide, but according to how many congressional districts the candidate wins. These districts having already been gerrymandered to favor Republicans; the proposal would allow a GOP candidate to win the lion's share of Virginia's electoral votes even while being soundly beaten in the popular vote.

For example, President Obama won Virginia's popular vote in 2012 and was awarded its thirteen electoral votes under the winner-take-all convention followed by all but three states. If the new scheme had been in place, he would have won only four of Virginia's thirteen electoral votes. While the authors of this measure later withdrew it under heavy criticism, I am not sure, as we get closer to the 2016 presidential contest, that GOP legislatures in key battleground states will not be tempted to place their thumbs on the scale in a similar fashion. As I write this, Republican lawmakers in Pennsylvania and Michigan are mulling over comparable ideas.

The already existing and always intensifying gerrymandering of seats for the House of Representatives practically ensures that Republicans will control that institution until the next census in 2020. Despite the fact that Republicans still have a 234–201 advantage in the House, GOP House candidates received almost a million and a half *fewer* votes in aggregate than Democratic candidates in 2012. Statistical oddities happen, of course, but they can also point to flaws in the electoral system. If you knew before the election that a million and a half more voters would chose Democratic candidates, then you would have given at least 24:1 odds that the Democrats would do better than 201 seats, so long as you knew that Democratic and Republican voters were fairly and randomly distributed across all congressional districts. In probability theory, this is the well-known "coin toss game." Twenty-four to one is not a freakish probability, unlike the odds of winning the Powerball jackpot, but it nevertheless points to structural biases in the way Americans are obliged to choose their leaders.

As the world's oldest continuous constitutional republic, our political system has many archaic and contradictory features that do not guarantee pure democracy. When there is a modus vivendi between the two parties, a sense of fair play generally dictates that the will of the people should prevail. But when one party becomes an ideological cult, as I believe the GOP has, it will cut every corner in its drive to achieve and maintain political power—the will of the actual majority of the American people be damned. Thus far, they haven't figured out how to gerrymander Senate races. I suppose that accounts for the intermittent fondness of Tea Party stalwarts for repealing the Seventeenth Amendment, which provides for the popular election of senators.

Thus, for structural reasons, the current GOP will not be disappearing anytime soon. Nor is it likely to modify its positions significantly. Even Governor Jindal has merely been talking about changing the messaging of the party rather than its platform; he thinks its core beliefs are sound. And while excoriating the Romney campaign's foolish public relations strategy of harping on the theme of "makers" versus "takers," Jindal's own fiscal proposals for Louisiana are cut from the same cloth. He wants to eliminate all state income taxes, which fall mainly on the well-to-do, and all corporate taxes. To replace them, he would increase regressive sales taxes, which mostly burden the middle class and working poor, in a state that is already sixth from the bottom in income inequality.

The GOP base, the people who show up for party primaries and conventions, is acting more and more like a conclave of conspiracy buffs, and the electoral defeat on November 6 did not dent their zeal. On December 4, 2012, the firm Public Policy Polling announced its survey findings: 49 percent of self-identified GOP voters think the progressive activist organization ACORN (Association of Community Organizations for Reform Now) stole the 2012 election for President Obama. This was a 3 percent drop from those who thought ACORN stole the 2008 election, but perhaps a more trifling decline than one might expect given the fact that ACORN had shut down in 2010!

It is this sort of conspiracy-laced thinking among the GOP base that drives many Republican officeholders to act as they do, particularly in the House. Thanks to gerrymandering, they need not fear defeat in a general election. But they must constantly be on guard against a Tea Party-inspired challenge from the right in a primary election. That explains why, in the January 1, 2013, vote to avert the "fiscal cliff," a substantial majority of Republican House members opposed the measure, just as they did in a later vote to provide relief for Hurricane Sandy victims. This dynamic guarantees there will be confrontation and gridlock over taxes, budgets, and virtually every other issue as far as the eye can see.

A somewhat different dynamic operates in the Senate, but there too, the pull is toward dysfunction, malgovernance, and juvenile grandstanding. In the last four years, President Obama has made many questionable decisions on foreign and national security policy whose implications the public needs to understand. The so-called senior statesmen of the Senate ought to be dispassionately examining these issues in the manner of the Fulbright hearings during the Vietnam War. Just a few of the administration's policies that urgently bear scrutiny: Was the overthrow of Libya's Moamar Ghaddafi a wise policy in view of the continuing destabilization of that country and the spread of instability to Mali? Is Libya a template for what could happen should the Syrian opposition overthrow the Assad regime? Is the administration's assassination-by-drone doctrine an effective means of combating terrorism, or does it spread terrorism by destabilizing countries like Yemen and nuclear-armed Pakistan? Are the problems of the Middle East even amenable to military force by an outside power?

If you expect plausible answers to any one of those questions from the Senate Foreign Relations Committee, the Senate Armed Services Committee, or from debate on the Senate floor, you will be waiting a long time. The hearings in early 2013 on the attack on the U.S. consulate in Benghazi and the confirmation of Secretary of Defense nominee Chuck Hagel were instead exercises in empty posturing, witness badgering, genuflecting to lobbies, and smug displays of know-nothingism.

By engaging in personal recriminations against Secretary Clinton and Hagel, Republican senators may have gotten themselves in solid with Rush Limbaugh. But once again, they actually did President Obama a favor by leaving the contradictions of his policies unexamined. By refusing to be a responsible opposition party, and instead simply being bomb-throwers, the Republican party has let Obama and the Democrats off the hook with respect to crucial foreign policy choices.

The same criticism applies to Obama's agenda here at home. Are you really reassured by Obama and his operatives' blithe assertions that your supposedly inalienable privacy rights under the Fourth Amendment can withstand the onslaught of the PATRIOT Act and the FISA amendments, particularly as those laws are being executed by reference to a whole library full of secret and unchallengeable executive orders? Why did his administration punt on any serious effort to stanch the hemorrhage of home foreclosures? Why did Democrats make the Affordable Care Act less affordable by mandating an enormous taxpayer giveaway to the pharmaceutical industry? And why did Obama extract no meaningful quid pro quo from financial entities receiving the largest bailout in history? Forget the small-fry crooks like Bernie Madoff: Why is not a single one of the really big Wall Street crooks in prison?

Where were the Republicans in questioning all these matters? Other than in a handful of sporadic performances, such as those of gadflies like Senator Rand Paul regarding the potential targeting of

U.S. citizens by drones, GOP officeholders remained silent.* Rather than being a vigorous but sane parliamentary opposition, they preferred to act like the caricature villain in a Victorian melodrama, twirling their mustaches as they expound on Kenyan socialism, legitimate rape, and death panels.

The problems this country faces are daunting, and neither party faces up to them. While Republicans refuse to acknowledge that we have a revenue problem, Democrats will not acknowledge a spending problem. And neither party, in a now-rare example of bipartisan agreement, acknowledges that the United States has, in its national security policy, an imperial overstretch problem. To put it bluntly, our entire national security establishment, including the fossilized congressional committees that give that establishment a blank check, is living in a fantasy world. It is difficult for us to impress other countries with our $10-billion aircraft carriers when we are in hock to those countries up to our eyeballs. In the long run, double-entry bookkeeping always trumps military glory.

Our challenges, however daunting, are hardly insoluble. Has any one of our self-styled statesmen given thoughtful consideration as to how recent discoveries of domestic energy, which may make the United States a net exporter of oil and gas by 2020, might free us from the Faustian bargain of our security guarantees to the oil-producing countries of the Middle East and the perpetual wars that go with them? Could high unemployment, an intractable merchan-

---

* Some of his Republican colleagues, like Senate Republican leader Mitch McConnell, indulged Paul's filibuster because it threw a monkey wrench into the administration's timing of John Brennan's confirmation as CIA director rather than as an expression of any belief in civil liberties. On the other hand, last-ditch Republican hawks like John McCain and Lindsey Graham petulantly derided Paul, apparently on the authoritarian principle that even to question the legal and ethical aspects of the national security state's authority to assassinate human beings was a form of lèse-majesté.

dise trade deficit, and the hollowing out of the U.S. industrial base all be redressed by the promotion of domestic manufacturing, as the Republican Party once advocated back in the nineteenth century? Could the money saved from endless wars and bribing foreign client states be better spent giving this country a public infrastructure worthy of the twenty-first century?

None of these solutions is impossible. But achieving them will require reorienting American politics away from serfdom to corporate money, the demands of the military-industrial complex, incitement by radio clowns, and the dead hand of discredited ideologies. And it will require a new and more serious attitude on the part of the American citizen. Politics is not the Army-Navy football game, still less the enthusiasm of the Roman mob for the chariot races in the Circus Maximus. It is the citizen's exercise of self-governance, which requires acquaintance with issues, resistance to distraction, and dispassionate immunity from the lures of party tribalism. The February 2013 Italian elections present a vivid if depressing example of what happens when the citizens of a country simply give up on responsible self-governance and instead treat politics like a reality TV show.

The reader may object that with all the structural rigidities in our political system, and above all the system's thralldom to money, how can the average citizen change things for the better? But American farmers, coal miners, and factory hands of a century ago, fed up with the raw deal the country's plutocrats handed them, raised enough hell that the system had to respond with antitrust statutes, wage-and-hour laws, pure food and drug regulations, and many other measures. Today's elected officials, just like those of the Gilded Age, typically show craven obedience to entrenched wealth. It is long past time that they show greater fear of a well-informed public capable of articulating its political demands.

THE PARTY IS OVER

INTRODUCTION

This book is about America's broken political system: how it got that way, who benefits, and who loses. It is about the growing domination of the legislative process by corporate money and the corresponding decline of a broad public interest. It is about how politicians use intensely polarizing ideological issues as bait to energize their political bases—and to divert those followers away from focusing on the one overriding political issue in our society: who gets what.

As America's political dysfunction has grown worse, the economic stagnation of the middle class has deepened. This is not a result of blind economic forces, Adam Smith's invisible hand, globalization, or some other nebulous cause. Specific committees of Congress, inevitably assisted by specific K Street lobbyists, wrote legislation that achieved this result.

Why am I so sure of what I say? I worked in Congress for twenty-eight years, most of the time as a professional staff member analyzing legislation for the House and Senate budget committees. For the first twelve years I worked for John Kasich, a Republican member of the House Armed Services Committee, and my fiefdom was national security. Then I switched to the House Budget Committee when Kasich became chairman. Finally, I moved to the Senate Budget Committee under the chairmanship of Senator Judd Gregg (R-New Hampshire). My duties gave me an invaluable perspective on government budgeting, and particularly on budgeting for national security. And they enabled me to understand that when politicians claim they will cut taxes, wage war around the planet, and balance the budget at the same time, they are spouting rank falsehoods. I was in the privileged position to see how Congress works on the inside, when the C-SPAN cameras are turned off. What I saw was not Civics 101 or *Jefferson's Manual* but an auction where political services are won by the highest bidder.

I was compelled to write this book because I became alarmed by the trends I was seeing. In particular, my own party, the Republican Party, began to scare me. After the 2008 election, Republican politicians became more and more intransigently dogmatic. They doubled down on advancing policies that transparently favored the top 1 percent of earners in this country while obstructing measures such as the extension of unemployment insurance. They seemed to want to comfort the comfortable and afflict the afflicted in the middle of the worst economic meltdown in eighty years.

And there was worse to come. Whether it was Representative Joe Wilson (R-South Carolina) boorishly yelling "You lie!"—unprecedented behavior during a joint meeting of Congress assembled to hear a presidential address—or the obscene carnival of birtherism, Obama-the-secret-Muslim, death panels, and all the rest of it, the party took on a nasty, bullying, crazy edge. From my vantage point on the budget committee I watched with a mixture of fascination and foreboding as my party was hijacked by a new crop of opportunists and true believers hell-bent on dragging the country into their jerry-built New Jerusalem: an upside-down utopia in which corporations rule; the Constitution, like science, is faith based; and war is the first, not the last, resort in foreign policy.

I suspect many of these politicians never believed what they were saying but were cynically playing to an increasingly deranged political base that *does* believe it. Television viewers could observe the outcome of this strategy in September 2011, when the partisan audience invited to view the Republican presidential candidates' debate at the Reagan Library in California cheered and clapped at the mentions of executions and the prospect of letting the uninsured die.

Do Democrats offer a sane alternative? The explanation is more complicated, but the answer is, finally, no. They have not become an extremist party like the GOP—their politicians do not match the current crop of zanies who infest the Republican Party—but their problem lies in the opposite direction. It is not that they are fanatics or zealots; it is that most do not appear to believe in *anything* very strongly. Democrats who expect this book to be a diatribe against Republicans alone will be disappointed. The GOP has gone off the rails—it is the party I know best, and which I will describe in greater detail. But its sorry situation is a symptom of a deeper dysfunction in American politics and society for which Democrats own a considerable share of the responsibility.

The Democratic Party coasted far too long on Franklin D. Roosevelt's legacy. It became complacent and began to feel entitled to its near hegemonic position in politics, culture, and the media. When the New Right increasingly began to displace it in all three of those arenas, some liberals merely turned into ineffectual whiners and crybabies or ivory tower escapists. The bulk of Democratic politicians and operatives, however, moved in a different direction. After three straight losses in presidential elections between 1980 and 1988, they abandoned the practices of their old beliefs while continuing to espouse them in theory. These new Democrats will say anything to win an election—an objective that, in their minds, generally requires them to emulate Republicans, particularly with respect to moneygrubbing on the fund-raising circuit. Many of them last only a term or two, because if people want a Republican, they will vote for the real thing. What has evolved in America over the last three decades is a one-and-a-half-party system, as Democrats opportunistically cleave to the "center," which, in the relativistic universe of American politics, keeps moving further to the right.

a significant paragraph

The current political dynamic is beginning to defeat the optimistic expectations of James Madison. As one of the chief architects of our federal system, Madison believed that competing factional interests would balance out one another, and that the government, like Newtonian clockwork, would keep on ticking. In times of general social harmony and tolerably shared prosperity, this theory worked well enough: Big business and big labor roughly balanced each other. But this balance has fallen terribly askew in the last thirty years. Unions ceased to be the political power and source of campaign funding they once were. Democrats increasingly turned to Wall Street and corporate America for handouts as the cost of elections kept rising. The legacy of this Faustian bargain is an ambivalent, hesitant, and split-minded party: still halfheartedly regarding itself as the party of the New Deal, the common man, the working stiff, but at the same time advancing the agenda of the corporate donors who call the shots. Money has overtaken politics so completely that factional interests are now simply competing to buy votes.

James Fallows has pointed out the shortcomings of the balance theory in the modern context: "The major parts of our political establishment are both showing operational pathologies that *each makes the other's failings worse*, rather than somehow buffering each other toward a harmonious best-of-both-worlds compromise result."[1] From what I have seen in Congress, Fallows is right: Whenever Democrats and Republicans achieve "bipartisan compromise," which generally happens when it comes time to restrict constitutional rights and put the next $100 billion installment for our endless wars on the national credit card, the public loses.

★

It has been little more than a decade since a secretary of state in a Democratic administration smugly declared that the United States was "the indispensable nation." Self-satisfied pundits extolled the United States not only as the sole remaining superpower but as a *hyperpower.* A few years after that, operatives in a Republican administration pronounced the invasion of Iraq "a cakewalk" and opined that the "Greater Middle East" was yearning for the healing touch of American liberators, armed to the teeth.

In the second decade of the twenty-first century, the American establishment's bipartisan vaunting and hubris have turned to ashes. It is not by happenstance that America today looks more like a Third World country than an advanced industrial state in international comparisons of social health such as longevity, infant mortality, income distribution, social mobility, labor protection, average number of vacation days, and many other metrics. Our tax policies have ensured that the rich got richer and the rest of us got stuck with the bill. Congressional obedience to corporatized medicine ensured that Americans pay an average of 50 percent more for their health care than citizens in Western Europe. Union busting, leveraged buyouts, and the offshoring of jobs guaranteed lower wages and fewer labor protections. According to the International Monetary Fund (IMF), China—Communist China!—is on track to have a gross domestic product greater than that of the United States by 2016.

In my early youth, when tail-finned Plymouths and porthole Buicks cruised the brick-paved streets of my midwestern hometown, we were told to clean our plates and not let the food go to waste. Had we no appreciation? There were starving children in Europe! Europe, mind you—which now has an aggregate GDP greater than that of the United States. As for China, it barely registered at the time. Chinese peasants in 1959 were eating tree bark and grass and living in little better than Bronze Age conditions courtesy of Chairman Mao and his Great Leap Forward. Now, thanks to the money men, arbitrageurs, buyout artists, and the politicians they rent, much of the former American industrial base resides in China.

Charles de Gaulle once said that the graveyards are full of indispensable men, and so it is with nations. As a historian by training, I have bad news for the political establishment in Washington: There is no divine plan guaranteeing America's global preeminence. There is also no divine plan mandating that the American middle class shall remain in existence forever. If the politicians running this country continue to pursue ideological chimeras and cater to the narrow, short-run desires of moneyed elites and extremist pressure groups while neglecting the broader national interest, we might as well resign ourselves to taking a place among the former great powers of history.

The downgrading of U.S. sovereign debt by Standard & Poor's during the summer of 2011 was an epochal event—the first credit downgrade of our nation since the ratings began in 1917. Read that credit report carefully. It was not a downgrade based on America's technical inability to redeem its debt instruments; it was primarily dictated by the political dysfunction in Washington and the expectation that things will not get better anytime soon. The rating agency turned out to be right: The ineffectuality of the so-called super committee (officially the Joint Select Committee on Deficit Reduction) a few months later, the payroll tax farce during the Christmas season, and the prospect of more government shutdowns to come plainly show that partisan rancor is making the day-to-day process of orderly governance impossible.

This breakdown is not unique in the world. Regardless of what the apostles of American Exceptionalism may say, the United States cannot isolate itself from the tide of international events. Our malaise is part of a global governance crisis and a breakdown of laissez-faire economics. Europe, once a nearly miraculous example of stability and prosperity after its phoenixlike rise from the ashes of World War II, is experiencing an existential turning point that will decide whether peaceful and democratic integration continues or the continent regresses to a cockpit of rivalry. Political change is sweeping North Africa and the Middle East—including in some of the states that have been clients of our fading global hegemony. Even the Russian people, assumed to have been resigned to the arctic chill of authoritarian "guided" democracy, have grown restless.

A warning about decline should not be a counsel of despair. A look at basic material factors will show that the United States is not in nearly as bleak a position as our present predicament suggests. It is a continent-sized country lying mostly in the temperate zone, bounded on two sides by the largest moats in the world. It has three hundred million inhabitants who can supply a tremendous pool of human capital. It has a greater quantity of productive arable land in a suitable climate than any other country and a staggering array of natural resources—both of which a wise government would use carefully as it stewards them for the benefit of generations unborn. Compared to Greece, a rocky southern outlier of the Balkan Mountains living on foreign tourism and controlling neither its currency nor its economic policy, the substantive difficulties of the United States are trivial. America's problems are at root political problems of our own making, the result of destructive habits of mind, and these factors are amenable to solutions we can devise.

According to a CBS/New York Times poll, Congress's favorability rating stands at 9 percent, the lowest since polling began.[2] Even the prospect of "America going communist" has higher public favorability, at 11 percent, than our legislative branch. Some of this cynicism and disenchantment is the result of deliberate political engineering to make Americans lose faith in their government, as we shall see later in this book. But Americans are angry all the same, and they have cause to be angry.

Political anger can be a constructive thing. Not the blind, unthinking anger of those who have been carefully worked into a perpetual rage by the expertly trained pitchmen of political talk radio, or the anger of the single-issue zealot or culture warrior, but the steady, rational indignation of the fully informed citizen about the fact that his rights and privileges are being usurped, and that his heritage is being squandered.

This is that story as I saw it unfold—the story of the seizure of our political system by special interests—and what I believe must be done to reverse this process.

1

THE PARTY OF LINCOLN, THE PARTY OF JEFFERSON

What is the Republican Party like? What are the Democrats like? Why is there so little difference between them? And how did they get this way?

☆ ☆ ☆

Barbara Stanwyck: "We're both rotten!"
Fred MacMurray: "Only you're a little
more rotten."

—*Double Indemnity* (1944)

Those lines of dialogue from a classic film noir sum up the state of the two political parties in contemporary America. Both parties are rotten—how could they not be? The complete infestation of the political system by corporate money now requires a presidential candidate to raise upward of a billion dollars to be competitive in the general election. But the parties are not rotten in quite the same ways. Democrats have their share of machine politicians, careerists, corporate bagmen, egomaniacs, and kooks. None of them, however, quite match the members of the modern GOP.

To those millions of Americans who watched with exasperation the tragicomedy of summer 2011's debt-ceiling extension crisis, it might have come as a shock that the Republican Party is so full of lunatics. To be sure, like any political party on Earth, the GOP has always had its share of crackpots, such as Robert K. Dornan or William E. Dannemeyer in past Congresses. But the crackpot outliers of two decades ago have become the vital core today: Eric Cantor, Steve King, Michele Bachmann, Paul Broun, Patrick McHenry, Virginia Foxx, Louie Gohmert, and Allen West. The *Congressional Directory* now reads like a casebook of lunacy. This is not to say that such specimens represent all or even most Republicans, but they have managed, through their shrillness, dogmatism, inflexibility, and belligerence, to become the center of gravity of the party. The Republican Speaker of the House, the constitutionally designated third-ranking elected official in the government, does not issue orders to them; he takes orders from them, as all of America saw during the debt-limit negotiations and the payroll tax fight.

It was this cast of characters and the pernicious ideas they represent that drove me to end a nearly thirty-year career in government: Last summer, I retired. I could see long before it happened that the Republican Party would use the debt-limit vote, an otherwise routine legislative procedure undertaken eighty-seven times since the end of World War II, to concoct an entirely artificial fiscal crisis. Then they would use that alleged fiscal crisis, literally holding the United States' and global economies hostage, to get what they wanted.

How did the Republican Party, the party of Lincoln, Theodore Roosevelt, Robert Taft, and Eisenhower, metamorphose into the intensely ideological, almost cultlike grouping of today? And how did it come to pass that the Democratic Party, the only other choice in America's ossified two-party political regime, should offer so little by way of an alternative?

★

When I entered government in the early 1980s, the Republican Party could plausibly represent itself as a pragmatic alternative to the Democrats, who still carried a stigma from the 1960s as a party of social engineering and ideological excess. The debacle of the 1968 Democratic presidential convention in Chicago, where riots broke out, led television viewers to conclude that the Democrats could no longer govern. Back then the GOP had a moderate wing of considerable influence. People such as Senator Howard Baker, who was known as "the Great Conciliator," and Representative Bob Michel (the Republican leader in the House) had stature in the party. These were politicians of the old school, who could reach across the aisle, make a deal, and stick to it. Ronald Reagan himself, the icon and dream figure of present-day Republicans, had little reluctance to negotiate over issues of taxing and spending, declare the resulting compromise a victory, and move on.

Bipartisan coalitions were still possible back then. My first job was as a legislative assistant for Representative Kasich, who was a strongly conservative fiscal hawk from my home state of Ohio. But he was able to join forces with Ron Dellums, then one of the most liberal Democrats in Congress, to propose limits on the production of the horrendously expensive B-2 bomber to save taxpayers billions of dollars. I knew, as a staff vote counter for the project, that their coalition was well on its way to getting the majority they would need to win if a vote was called. Apparently the vote counters at the Pentagon came to the same conclusion: The Department of Defense killed further production of B-2s to avoid an embarrassing vote on the floor of the House. Congressional coalitions of this type are nearly extinct today. The only thing remotely similar since the 2008 election has been the quixotic antiwar alliance between Ron Paul and Dennis Kucinich, but both are pariahs in their own parties and rarely muster more than a handful of votes in favor of their proposals. And Kucinich, redistricted out of his congressional seat, will not be returning to Congress after the 2012 election.

The GOP has been gradually shedding its status as a broad coalition party and has started demanding litmus tests on fiscal, social, and foreign policy issues. There were signposts on the road ahead—the Gingrich revolution of 1995, the Clinton impeachment circus—but things got much worse after September 11, with the massive infringements of civil liberties that followed and the bluster and bravado that preceded the invasion of Iraq. By the 2010 midterm election the party had collectively lost its mind. The evidence is all around us: the debt ceiling debacle, the kamikaze politics over the payroll tax cut extension, the freak show of the Republican presidential debates. How did this happen?

Under the influence of political consultants such as Karl Rove, the GOP decided that educated and affluent (but not necessarily rich) suburban voters could be taken for granted to vote for them as the "natural governing party." The party could thus focus on gaining new adherents by sharpening its differences with the opposition. They soon discovered that they could accomplish this by promoting divisive "culture wars," and turned their focus to issues such as abortion and gay marriage. Party operatives sought to paint the Democrats as appeasers—weak on defense and uninterested in keeping the American people safe. They attacked them as faithless namby-pambys, urban elites who were out of touch with the American heartland. Their strategy reaped dividends—in 1994, Republicans captured both the House and Senate for the first time in forty years, for a twelve-year run—and it led to the party's fielding new candidates who were rabidly zealous on these issues, among others. The GOP fell increasingly under the influence of theocratic fundamentalists eager to use the resources of the state to regulate private behavior, and of neoconservative chicken hawks—some of them ex-Democrats—who never saw a war they didn't want somebody else's kid to fight.

Republicans have traditionally been more solicitous toward the interests of the wealthy and their enterprises than their Democratic counterparts—though this did not prevent Dwight Eisenhower from seeking to maintain a high marginal tax rate on the wealthy or Ronald Reagan from saying that wages should not be taxed at a higher rate than capital. But the party has increasingly, and with single-minded focus since Barack Obama's election, devoted itself exclusively to the interests of the wealthy. Knowing that the remaining 99 percent of the population would have a hard time becoming enthusiastic over a party platform that nakedly proclaimed itself devoted to the advancement of the rich, the GOP has confected a shrewd marketing campaign: play up the culture wars and demagogue national security issues to distract voters from their real intentions. It did not take long for clever political consultants to realize that, in the absence of critical and analytical news media, the most assertive and repetitive voice will win the argument. Also, the GOP reflexively scorns so-called elites (by which it means educated, critical thinkers) to mask the way it is utterly beholden to the true American elite: the plutocracy that runs the country.

I would like to be able to contrast this characterization with a positive one of the Democrats, the supposed party of the people, to make this book a neat and simple morality tale. But the Democrats at this time offer only a weak and tepid alternative. Why? They are also in the tank with wealthy contributors.

Democrats expressed outrage, and justifiably so, at the sole-source contracts the Bush administration gave to Halliburton after the invasion of Iraq, but what do they say now about the loan guarantees the Obama administration granted to Solyndra, a now de-

HALIBURTON IS NOT DEFUNCT

funct solar power company whose campaign donations flowed to
the Democratic Party? *BAD COMPERISON*

★

In its *Citizens United* decision in 2010, the Supreme Court ruled
that corporations could spend unlimited amounts to influence
elections, equating corporate money with free speech. The usual
flood of money into Washington has since become an uncontrol-
lable torrent. This further loosening of restrictions on fund-raising
engendered the creation of so-called super PACs, whose donors
can remain anonymous. Just one of these super PACs, Karl Rove's
American Crossroads, expects to raise $250 million for the 2012
elections.

We may soon be on the verge of building the perverse utopia
envisioned by the reactionary billionaire H. L. Hunt in the 1960s.
Hunt, who won the deed to a huge stake in the East Texas oil fields
in a poker game in 1930, attributed his wealth not just to a bit of
luck and business acumen, but to his own unique moral and civic
virtue. After funding the right-wing senator Joe McCarthy and the
John Birch Society in the 1950s, he turned to more visionary projects. In his 1960 vanity-published book *Alpaca* he limned what he
held to be an ideal society: one that grants the wealthy more votes
than citizens of modest means.

The *Citizens United* decision has brought the country closer to
Hunt's plutocratic utopia than we've ever been. And it has brought
the Supreme Court itself back to the mental atmosphere of the
1886 Court, when a headnote—a comment not written by one of
the justices—of the opinion in a case, *Santa Clara County v. Southern Pacific Railroad*, laid the foundation of "corporate personhood"
and established the precedence of corporate prerogatives over citizens' rights. In those days, though, the citizenry was made of

tougher stuff. A vigorous third-party movement arose to challenge the decision. Though the People's Party ("Populists") did not achieve national power in its own right, it mobilized public opinion behind a reform movement to roll back the oligarchs' privileges. And it was at least partially successful. Its 1892 Omaha platform called out the highest court, along with the rest of the political apparatus, as rotten:

> We meet in the midst of a nation brought to the verge of moral, political, and material ruin. Corruption dominates the ballot-box, the Legislatures, the Congress, and touches even the ermine of the bench. The people are demoralized. . . . The newspapers are largely subsidized or muzzled, public opinion silenced, business prostrated, homes covered with mortgages, labor impoverished, and the land concentrating in the hands of capitalists. The urban workmen are denied the right to organize for self-protection, imported pauperized labor beats down their wages. . . . The fruits of the toil of millions are boldly stolen to build up colossal fortunes for a few, unprecedented in the history of mankind, and the possessors of these, in turn, despise the Republic and endanger liberty. From the same prolific womb of governmental injustice we breed the two great classes—tramps and millionaires.

While the Populists disappeared a few years later, much of their platform found its way into the programs of the Democratic Party and the progressive wing of the GOP under Theodore Roosevelt. Our progressive income tax system, the direct election of senators, and antitrust laws are just a few of their legacies.

Our party duopoly is one of the most locked-in and rigged systems among the nations that are commonly thought of as the Western democracies. It is next to impossible now for any third party to break into this system in the way the then new third-party Republicans did in the 1850s, though many have tried. And even that example does not tell the whole story: The 1850s Republicans basically picked up the torch from the antislavery wing of the dying Whig Party. We have never had three viable parties at any one time in over two hundred years.

The Democrats and the GOP, on both the federal and state levels, are in various disguised ways written into electoral law (a practice finding no support in the Constitution), and this contrivance presents a decisive hurdle against almost all new entrants. Democrats and Republicans are almost automatically on the ballot. Third-party candidates, by contrast, must overcome onerous petition requirements, and since the state legislatures that set the qualifying regulations and draw up the voting districts are occupied exclusively by Democrats and Republicans, those who are dissatisfied with both parties are effectively disenfranchised.

As a practical matter, voters can only express dissatisfaction with the established party that happens to be in power by voting for the other established party. In 2006 and 2008, voters were angry with the Republicans, so they voted for the Democrats. Then, in 2010, they were angry with the Democrats, so they voted for the GOP. What they will do in 2012 is an open question. But we can be sure of one thing: Regardless of who wins in November 2012, the campaign for the 2014 congressional elections will begin on the day after the vote, and by January 2013 we shall start hearing about likely prospects for the 2016 presidential contest. The United States is unique in that it operates in permanent campaign mode; campaign seasons in most European countries are limited by law to a few weeks or months.

The shortcomings of the American electoral system are

thrown into ironic relief whenever the international arms of the two main parties, the National Democratic Institute (NDI) and the International Republican Institute (IRI), scold some foreign country for its political misdeeds. Yes, you read that right: The two parties have international offshoots operating abroad. Although organized as nonprofit entities legally separate from their parent parties, they carry those parties' ideological baggage much as the Comintern was the cat's-paw of the Soviet Communist Party. And they are funded by your tax dollars: Both NDI and IRI are categorized as 501(c)3 "charitable" organizations by the Internal Revenue Service, but they receive the vast bulk of their money not from private donors, who can consequently take tax deductions, but from federal funds appropriated to official government entities such as the State Department, the United States Agency for International Development, and the National Endowment for Democracy.

And what do these august bodies do, aside from supplying résumé-building slots for party operatives and board memberships for partisan officeholders burnishing their credentials as statesmen? While they are forbidden by law from providing direct funding to foreign political parties (that would be too much like the old days, when the CIA funneled subsidies through fake foundations to favored parties abroad), they accomplish nearly the same result by indirect support through get-out-the-vote strategies, "voter education," election monitoring, or favorable international publicity for the political party they prefer.

In 2011, both organizations criticized Ukraine for inhibiting new political parties' access to the ballot. How Ukraine's system differs from our own practices that restrict third-party ballot access is unclear. They also criticized Ukraine for having a system of plurality victors with no subsequent run-off vote. Again, it is not obvious how this differs from our own system: One has only to glance back to the American presidential elections of 1992 and 1996, when the winner did not gain a majority of the popular vote, not to mention that of 2000, when the candidate with fewer votes than his major party competitor went on to become president.

Whether and how to increase access to the ballot for third parties is a complex problem, and efforts to solve it could have many unintended consequences. The same applies to rules governing how elections are decided or how electoral districts should be determined. But for the international arms of our two political parties—dependent on government funds as they are—to complain when other countries practice what has long been established here by law is a uniquely American characteristic: a blindness about the supposed perfection of our venerable democratic system of governance married to a habit of lecturing everybody under the sun. It is the same hypocrisy and arrogance that is regularly on display when the secretary of state condemns other countries for practicing torture or involvement in extrajudicial killings.

★

The police and petty bureaucrats in many Third World countries are openly corrupt and will take bribes in order to augment their miserable salaries. In the United States it is relatively difficult to bribe a cop to get out of a traffic ticket or to slip money to a DMV functionary to get preferential treatment. You need to go higher up the governmental food chain in order to practice corruption successfully. But you can find bribery and corruption just about anytime, year-round, in Washington. It is called a fund-raiser, when a congress member's campaign committee rents a room in a restaurant and invites a hundred or so of his or her closest friends from the lobbying shops on K Street, from industry, and from the trade associations. I've been to a few of these over the years and often wondered whether any of the Gucci-shod participants in their two-thousand-dollar suits and monogrammed shirts imagined that they were righteously engaged in the constitutional practice of petitioning for the redress of grievances as they handed over their checks before tucking into the hors d'oeuvres.

Bill Moyers has denounced these activities as money laundering, and paints an equally unflattering portrait of each party:

> John Boehner calls on the bankers, holds out his cup, and offers them total obeisance from the House majority if only they fill it. That's now the norm, and they get away with it. GOP once again means Guardians of Privilege. Barack Obama criticizes bankers as "fat cats," and then invites them to dine at a pricey New York restaurant, where the tasting menu runs to $195 a person. That's now the norm, and they get away with it. The president has raised more money from banks, hedge funds, and private equity managers than any Republican candidate, including Mitt Romney. Inch by inch he has conceded ground to them while espousing populist rhetoric that his very actions betray.[1]

During the last thirty years, the American political system has been growing ever more dysfunctional as the cost of entry for candidates has become higher and higher. The election of 1980, when John Anderson received a respectable number of votes, may have been the last time a third-party candidate without lavish financing will have been able to do even moderately well in a presidential contest. (Ross Perot's challenge in 1992 was only feasible because he was a billionaire who could self-fund his campaign.) It is not a coincidence that as more and more money has infected the two parties, their concern for the well-being of the vast majority of the American people has declined. The expensive political ads that pollute television after Labor Day during an election year may ooze with empathy for Joe Average, but actions speak louder than words.

It is no coincidence that as the Supreme Court has been removing the last constraints on the legalized corruption of politicians, the American standard of living has been falling at the fastest rate in decades. According to the *Christian Science Monitor*, the average individual now has $1,315 less in disposable income than he or she did three years ago, at the onset of the Great Recession at the beginning of 2008.[2] This is not only a decline when measured against our own past economic performance; it also represents a decline relative to other countries, a far cry from the post–World War II era, when the United States had by any measure the highest living standard in the world. A study by the Bertelsmann Foundation concluded that in measures of economic equality, social mobility, and poverty prevention, the United States ranks twenty-seventh out of the thirty-one advanced industrial nations belonging to the Organization for Economic Cooperation and Development. Thank God we are still ahead of Turkey, Chile, and Mexico![3]

But what does some European foundation know? The Congressional Budget Office (CBO), Congress's own budget score-keeping and economic analysis arm, which is regarded as nonpartisan and objective, reported in October 2011 that the richest 1 percent of U.S. households had doubled their share of gross income from 10 percent to 20 percent since 1979, while that of everyone else had gone down.[4] Ironically, the same day the CBO released its report, Representative Paul Ryan (R-Wisconsin), the chairman of the House Budget Committee, was reminding us yet again that even the tepid rhetoric and timid policies of President Obama amounted to "class warfare," and that Republican policies would preserve "equality of opportunity. . . . Telling people they are stuck in their current station in life, that they are victims of circumstances beyond their control, and that the government's role is to help them cope with it—well, that's not who we are."

I should say it certainly is not. But who exactly are they, then? At the same time the CBO issued its report and Ryan made his speech, GOP presidential candidate Herman Cain was surging in popularity among the Republican base. Cain's claim to fame was a tax plan even more regressive than the current revenue system, which already taxes labor more heavily than capital; his jobs policy was a model of businesslike concision: "If you don't have a job, blame yourself!"

In the midst of the greatest and most protracted economic slump in eighty years, Cain's quip was similar in spirit to the proposal suggested by Andrew K. Mellon, President Herbert Hoover's secretary of the treasury, for dealing with the Great Depression—with the same dash of Calvinistic disdain for the destitute:

> Liquidate labor, liquidate stocks, liquidate the farmers, liquidate real estate. . . . It will purge the rottenness out of the system. High costs of living and high living will come down. People will work harder, live a more moral life. Values will be adjusted, and enterprising people will pick up the wrecks from less competent people.[5]

What America first experienced as tragedy the present generation must relive as farce.

Let us now dispose of the quaint notion that the present-day Republican Party is conservative. It has no vestige of conservatism as I once knew it, meaning prudence, caution, the tried and tested. The 1950s, when a Republican president occupied the White House, was a period of substantial real economic growth and shared prosperity—along with a 91 percent top marginal tax rate on individual incomes, while corporate tax revenues were a markedly higher share of total federal revenue than today. President Eisenhower denounced attempts to reduce the tax rates as fiscally irresponsible. In view of the current $15 trillion national debt, perhaps Ike was right after all. Can one imagine a Republican officeholder today advocating Eisenhower's tax policies?

A seemingly trivial but telling clue that the Republican Party is no longer a conservative but rather a radical right-wing party lies in the popular choice of colors to denote the two parties. It may not have been a conscious decision, but it is in retrospect appropriate that during the 2000 election all the television networks settled on red for the GOP and blue for the Democrats. Since the French Revolution, red has consistently been the emblem of upheaval and disruption in Western nations. Blue was just as surely associated with conservatism and tradition. The traditional psychology of colors in areas of life outside politics would seem to confirm this choice. Corporate directors do not wear red pinstriped suits to connote solidity, trustworthiness, and a reliable dividend for shareholders. Only blue will do, for red is the color of instability and change. "Better dead than red!" used to be the conservatives' motto.

How is it that the media upended this social convention in 2000 with its selection of colors to designate states on studio graphics? Why do self-described conservatives now proudly proclaim themselves as "red," or "red staters"? By the 2000 election, and certainly after 9/11, the Republican Party was no longer a conservative party in the traditional sense, as that word has been understood in Western political culture. Its belief in polarizing language and tactics, a militant and militarized foreign policy, and a constant search for mortal enemies, foreign and domestic alike, qualifies the current GOP as a radical right-wing party, not a conservative one. In his flawed but occasionally insightful book *Democracy and Populism: Fear and Hatred*, historian John Lukacs reminds us that "right wing" is not a synonym for conservative, and is not even a true variant of conservatism, although the right wing will opportunistically borrow conservative themes as the need arises. Hence, red is an appropriate color for a radical party like the present-day GOP.

But isn't that clue contradicted by Republicans' constant invocation of a "better" America that supposedly existed in the past, along with their appeal to traditional values that our ancestors allegedly kept better than we do? One branch of the American so-called conservative movement, the paleoconservatives, has honed this fetish for a lost Arcadia to an almost comic extent.* As the images of imagined pasts are sullied by some ideological defect, the paleocons keep pushing further back into the mists of time. The 1950s of *Ozzie and Harriet*, which most conventional right-wingers see in a nostalgic soft focus, was spoiled for paleoconservatives by the statist legacy of FDR. Most paleos have settled on pre–Civil War America as the golden age of their imaginations. Scratch many a paleoconservative and you will find a neo-Confederate at heart.

This romanticization of an idealized time, coupled with a ruthless leveling of traditional institutions, such as Medicare, the departments of energy and education, and the regulatory framework that has been around since the Progressive Era, has been an ever-present feature of radical right-wing movements during the twentieth century. Republican figures such as Sarah Palin, who appeal to a backward-looking "real" America in their rhetoric, somehow manage to reconcile themselves to the less romantic destruction of

---

* Some of the paleoconservatives, such as Pat Buchanan, are Republican partisans, while others profess to be alienated from electoral politics altogether, ostensibly because the Republican Party is too liberal for them.

tradition and social stability by laissez-faire capitalism. Let's face it: The Republican Party is no longer a broad-based conservative party in the historically accepted sense. It is an oligarchy with a well-developed public relations strategy designed to soothe and anesthetize its followers with appeals to tradition, security, and family even as it pursues a radical agenda that would transform the country into a Dickensian corporatocracy at home and a belligerent military empire abroad.

Against that radical Republican program the Democrats offer . . . nothing much at all. And from time to time, as we shall see, they reinforce the agenda of those who are ostensibly their opponents.

★

That is the Republican Party as I experienced it and the Democratic Party as I saw it at a slight distance. After the 2010 midterm election I felt the time had come for me to say good-bye to all that. There were too many logical contradictions and moral conflicts. All professional careers have their ups and downs, and on the whole, mine was a successful one that I could leave without regret or rancor. I made many good friends on the Hill, and I departed the institution on good terms with everyone. No doubt I have fewer friends now; so be it. But this book is not a confessional about personalities or relationships. It is an explanation, based on what I saw, of the dysfunction in our political system, and an assessment of what it means for our domestic prosperity, our constitutional freedoms, and our future standing in the world.

2

TACTICS: WAR MINUS THE SHOOTING

The Republican Party has used objection, obstruction, and filibustering not only to block the necessary processes of government but also in order to make ordinary Americans deeply cynical about Washington. Republicans perpetually run against government and come out on top. But, in the process, they are undermining the foundations of self-rule in a representative democracy.

★ ★ ☆

All men can see these tactics whereby I conquer, but what none can see is the strategy out of which victory is evolved.

—Sun Tzu

If the American people were interested in discovering the real reasons why they are so disenchanted with government, they would do well to focus less on the campaign horse race and the personality quirks of individual candidates and more on how laws are made and the tactics used by both parties to gain parliamentary advantage. Far from being boring high school Civics 101 stuff, this is the mechanism by which governance happens—or, increasingly, does not happen.

The U.S. Senate has more complex procedural rules than any

other legislative body in the world; many of these rules are contradictory, and on any given day the Senate parliamentarian may issue a ruling that contradicts earlier rulings on analogous cases. The only thing that can keep the Senate functioning is collegiality and good faith. During periods of political consensus, such as we experienced during World War II and immediately after the war, the Senate is generally a high-functioning institution: Filibusters are rare, and the body is legislatively productive. But when there is no consensus, it is practically a miracle if any major legislation is passed. One can no more picture our current Senate producing the original Medicare act than one can imagine the Supreme Soviet passing the Bill of Rights.

Almost every bill, nominee for Senate confirmation, and routine procedural motion is nowadays subject to a Republican filibuster. It is no wonder that Washington is gridlocked: Legislating has become war minus the shooting, much as it was eighty years ago in the Weimar Republic. As Hannah Arendt observed then, a disciplined totalitarian minority can use the instruments of democratic government to undermine democracy itself. Something along these lines is at work nowadays on Capitol Hill.

During the 112th Congress obstructionism reached the level of hostage taking every few months. Everyone knows that in a hostage situation, the reckless and amoral actor has the upper hand in the negotiations, because the cautious and responsible actor is concerned about the life of the hostage, while the former does not care. The debt-ceiling extension is not the only recent example of this sort of political terrorism. Republicans were willing to lay off four thousand Federal Aviation Administration employees and seventy thousand private construction workers, and to let FAA safety inspectors work without pay—in fact, to force them to pay for their own work-related travel; how prudent is that?—in order to strong-arm some union-busting provisions into the FAA reauthorization.

The GOP's thirst for confrontation and crisis is symptomatic of a destructive and nihilistic streak that has overtaken our political system. When one party repudiates the whole concept of compromise, it is inevitable that the government will lurch from one crisis to another. Long gone are the days of cautious and prudential conservatism. Observing the Republican obstruction during the debt-ceiling crisis of summer 2011, John B. Judis summed up the modern GOP this way:

> Over the last four decades, the Republican Party has transformed from a loyal opposition into an insurrectionary party that flouts the law when it is in the majority and threatens disorder when it is the minority. It is the party of Watergate and Iran-Contra, but also of the government shutdown in 1995 and the impeachment trial of 1999. If there is an earlier American precedent for today's Republican Party, it is the antebellum Southern Democrats of John Calhoun who threatened to nullify, or disregard, federal legislation they objected to, and who later led the fight to secede from the union over slavery.[1]

It is a truism that most people, whatever their trade or profession, want to believe that they are engaged in a useful and socially constructive endeavor, that given the option they would like to be proud of where they work and what they do. A couple of years ago a Republican committee staff director told me candidly (and proudly) that there was a method to all this obstruction and disruption. Should Republicans succeed in preventing the Senate from doing its job, it would further lower Congress's favorability rating among

the American people. In such a scenario the party that presents itself as programmatically against government—i.e., the Republican
Party—will come out the relative winner. As someone who came to
Washington believing that it was a privilege to do the public's business on Capitol Hill, I found this admission—or, rather, boast—
troubling.

The GOP has become more open about this tactic in recent
months. In January 2012, House Republican leader Eric Cantor informed the press that tax and health care legislation would be decided by the election. What he was really saying was that all
legislation on taxes or health care—both central to improving the
economic climate in the most severe and protracted period of economic distress since World War II—were off the table before November 2012. The media were too obtuse to notice that this was not
a case of Congress not being able to get its act together. It was a case
of the House Republican leader saying he would obstruct major
legislation that might affect our economic recovery for an entire
congressional session.

It was not always thus. In the 1980s, when I came to Washington, disposition of legislation was markedly less partisan than is
the norm today. To give an example I am familiar with, let's take a
quick look at the House and Senate conference to reconcile their
respective defense authorization bills to establish our military policy. (During the time Representative Kasich was on the Armed
Services Committee, I had a chance to watch the process up close.)
In general, members of the House and the Senate defended their
versions of the bill in conference regardless of their party. Thus,
the division of opinion, once a bill had reached the conference
committee, tended to be House versus Senate rather than Democrat versus Republican. There were significant exceptions, of
course, but the usual practice was to hash out a piece of legislation

that the president would sign, rather than using the bill as a vehicle for press releases and ideological posturing. The latter is the norm today. These days the resulting piece of legislation is loaded with policy riders to rev up the parties' political bases—believe it or not, abortion amendments are often inserted in defense authorization bills—and it generally arrives on the president's desk several months late.

In those halcyon days of Reagan's America that our current crop of Republicans so love to invoke, conference committees had a markedly different feel from those of today. Select members of the respective House and Senate committees came together in an effort to produce a compromise measure that they could actually send to the president in the expectation that he would sign it. There were plenary sessions with all, or most, members in attendance during which points of difference were debated and motions that might satisfy both sides were offered. It was generally businesslike, as people concentrated on resolving substantive matters.

Thanks to the Gingrich revolution of the mid-1990s, most of today's rare conference committee meetings have all the substance and spontaneity of a North Korean party congress. Their sole purpose is to allow both sides to make statements to the press during which they hit on all the familiar talking points. The real issues are resolved informally between the committee chairs of the House and Senate committees, and those chairs themselves are usually errand boys for the positions of the Speaker of the House and the majority leader of the Senate. The whole system has become a parody of the legislative process.

Barry Goldwater, who was a senior Republican on the Senate Armed Services Committee when I started out on the Hill, and whom many regarded as an ideologue, was far less ideological than the average member of Congress today. He wouldn't have dreamed of issuing a partisan jeremiad against his senior Democratic counterpart on the House Armed Services Committee, Bill Nichols of Alabama, let alone of campaigning against him. Barry was a crotchety old bird, but by then his principal preoccupation was reforming the Department of Defense rather than advancing an ideological agenda.

His cause in the mid-1980s was solving the systemic problems in DOD that he believed to be responsible for the catastrophic handling of the bombing of the Marine barracks in Beirut in October 1983. The hearings he called for, and parallel ones in the House, revealed a riot of military disorganization that rivaled that of the Crimean War: an unclear chain of command; almost nonexistent communications between the military services; vague rules of engagement; and poor coordination, even in the timely evacuation of the wounded. Goldwater and Nichols, both veterans with a deep understanding of the military, took the lead on investigating these debacles.

Goldwater and Nichols's subsequent determination to overhaul the military command structure took shape through legislative drafts in their respective houses of Congress. I was in many of those meetings and do not recall any partisan rancor among the members; the main opposition came from elements in DOD. Admiral James D. Watkins, the chief of naval operations, denounced the ultimate measure (much of which had been drafted by Nichols) as "un-American." Bill Nichols, a genteel and unfailingly courteous southerner who had lost a leg in the Battle of the Hürtgen Forest in World War II, was distinctly unamused. John Kasich was equally unamused, as he regarded Nichols as a friend and mentor. Can anyone imagine a mentor-protégé relationship across the aisle now? Because of these strong bipartisan loyalties, Admiral Watkins was briskly sent packing, and the legislation proceeded to passage and was signed into law by the president.

The passage of time may have smoothed some of the rougher edges off my recollections. The 1980s were not a golden era of legislation, to be sure, and military historians will judge whether the Goldwater-Nichols Department of Defense Reorganization Act of 1986 achieved any significant or lasting improvement in military performance. But what it demonstrated to a young staffer was that partisan considerations could be moderated in matters of national importance, and members of Congress were then far less overawed by the military brass than they are now. In recent years, as Vietnam has ceased to be a living memory for many new members of Congress, both parties have learned to genuflect to the judgments of "commanders in the field," even when the services presided over disasters or scandals.

An instructive contrast is offered by the legislative response almost two decades later to an even greater disaster than the Beirut bombing. After the September 11, 2001, terrorist attacks, the creation of the Department of Homeland Security was as much a legislative mess as it was an enduring monument to American gullibility and deliberately induced fearfulness. President Bush and his advisers, meaning Dick Cheney, did not want a cabinet department at first. Bush and Cheney preferred to keep homeland security functions under the executive office of the president, which would have made it free of legislative branch oversight.

When the cry from the Hill for a cabinet department became too distracting, the administration sent formal and informal legislative proposals to the Hill and bent the eventual result to its liking. In the face of all of its rhetoric about national unity (a concept that proved as fleeting as the rhetoric was mendacious and manipulative) the Bush crowd was determined to insert extraneous and divisive antiunion provisions into the legislation affecting employees of the new department. Unlike Admiral Watkins's extemporaneous rant in 1986, this was a coordinated ideological effort devised in tandem by the executive branch and congressional Republicans. The provisions had nothing to do with protecting the country from those whom President Bush liked to describe as "evildoers."

Some Democrats balked, including Max Cleland, a Democratic senator from Georgia. He was rewarded by Republicans on the Hill not with solidarity or understanding but with calumny. During the 2002 campaign for his Senate seat, his Republican opponent ran political ads suggesting that Cleland was aiding Osama bin Laden by opposing the antiunion provisions in the homeland security bill. Partly on the strength of those ads, his opponent, Saxby Chambliss, then a member of the House, won the election.

Like Nichols, Cleland was a war veteran, although his war was Vietnam. Like Nichols, he had lost a limb as a result of his service. He was in fact a triple amputee and had won a Silver Star and a Bronze Star for his service. His successor, the flag-waving Chambliss, avoided Vietnam thanks to five student deferments and a 1Y deferment owing to a well-timed knee injury sustained playing football. Ever the good Republican, Chambliss described his victory to his followers thus: "You have delivered tonight a strong message to the world that in conservative Georgia values matter." How did this country reach a point of such political and moral degradation that a demagogic draft evader could successfully defame a gravely wounded veteran over a red herring, when the country was supposedly united in its determination to heal the wounds of 9/11?

The answer: tactics, tactics, tactics.

★

To understand how hyperbolic partisanship, scorched-earth campaigns, and propaganda trumping legislation have gridlocked

Congress to the point of systemic dysfunction, it is useful to examine the meteoric career of Newton Leroy McPherson Gingrich.

Newt came to Washington in 1979, a few years before me, and by the time I arrived he was a rising star in the House Republican delegation. His bomb-throwing tactics and expert use of C-SPAN as free political advertising made him stand out from most of the other younger members of Congress. It was clear from the beginning that he was practicing a New Politics, hard-right version, but Newt really came into his own during the Clinton presidency, when he issued his "Contract with America," became the Speaker of the House, and spearheaded an aggressive showdown with the president over the budget in 1995. In 1996, after a year of legislative chaos and government shutdowns, and during which the country descended into virtual warfare between the House and the president under his speakership, I remarked to one of my colleagues that Newt would make a lousy George Washington, but he was one hell of a Robespierre.

It is often said of flawed judicial nominees that they lack a judicial temperament. But with the appropriate adjustments this critique could also be applied to other offices. People either have the temperament to legislate and govern, or they do not. George Washington is one of history's few examples of a man who could both lead a revolutionary effort and consolidate his political gains to help establish a stable and enduring governing structure. Robespierre was his polar opposite: brilliant at destroying the status quo but unable to temper his revolutionary impulses, and thus ultimately unable to rule. It wasn't long before his bold new order collapsed into military dictatorship.

Gingrich had few legislative accomplishments to point to from the sixteen years he spent in Congress prior to becoming Speaker of the House. I cannot recall any important bill that he inspired (unlike fellow activist Dick Armey, who worked hard to get his military base closure measure adopted, or Kasich, who successfully pushed through several measures on military reform and curbing government waste), or any significant activity in his committee assignments. The committee is where members of Congress are supposed to develop issue expertise, but Gingrich, the idea man, was above such mundane toiling.

His genius lay in recognizing the demagogic potential of the House's 1979 decision to televise its proceedings gavel to gavel. While most others saw this as at best a boring civics lesson, and at worst as a TV test pattern with occasional movement, Gingrich the old history teacher recognized that it would give him a chance to broadcast his political message nationwide, free of charge, to anyone who tuned in. He was relatively uninterested in participating in debates connected with the real business of Congress: measures that authorized or appropriated funds for the operation of government. Instead, he was the first to exploit the dead time after the completion of legislative business but before the cameras went dark to make so-called special order addresses to the C-SPAN camera before an empty chamber.

Using this free megaphone Gingrich and his two cohorts, Vin Weber and Bob Walker, launched the present era of over-the-top, confrontational, media-centric politics. They lashed out at Democrats as appeasement-minded socialist fellow travelers: For starters, they were criminally negligent for failing to confront the existential threat to America from the tiny nation of Nicaragua. The House, as Gingrich saw it, was a rotten, corrupt institution largely because it was run by Democrats.

All this might have remained a minor nuisance had not the Democratic Speaker, Tip O'Neill, on one occasion directed the

C-SPAN cameras to pan the empty seats in the House chamber when Gingrich or one of his sidekicks was speaking. He sought to undermine the trio, whom he called the Three Stooges, by showing that they were addressing a deserted assembly. They instantly fought back, claiming that they were deliberately being singled out, since other members had also availed themselves of special order speeches to pontificate before an empty chamber. Most important, the resulting controversy got Gingrich and his friends the attention they craved.

The Democrats, fat and lazy after nearly three continuous decades in control of the House, didn't know how to react. Gingrich quickly seized the reins. He made hay out of the 1983 congressional sex-with-pages scandal, and in 1988 he filed an ethics complaint against the then Speaker, Jim Wright, over improper payments for a book contract (Gingrich would later be charged with similar irregularities in his own book deal). Wright stepped down, and Gingrich advanced in the ranks of the Republican leadership. Then he ranted against the unacceptable bookkeeping practices of the House bank even though he himself had kited checks. Newt was learning that relentless attack is its own Teflon.

When Republicans won control of the House in 1994, Speaker Gingrich turned the institution upside down. He ended office deliveries of buckets of ice and engaged in dozens of comparable examples of perverse and inane micromanagement, such as renaming several of the committees to suit his own visionary taste. His "reform" merely resulted in money wasted junking and reprinting stationery and committee nameplates. He slashed the funding for what was then called the General Accounting Office (now the Government Accountability Office), Congress's watchdog agency, due to his belief that it was somehow a Democrat-leaning organization, although even arch–deficit hawk Senator Tom Coburn later said that the GAO provides ninety dollars in savings recommendations for every one dollar spent to fund the agency.

When a coup takes place in a banana republic, the new potentate renames the streets and plazas and redesigns the national flag. A similar narcissistic idiosyncrasy seemed to govern Newt's edicts. In the first year of his speakership, as I scrambled with fellow staffers on the House Budget Committee to put together the congressional budget resolution for committee consideration in the small hours of the morning, down came another edict from the Speaker: Rewrite it presenting the numbers differently. He wanted to disguise the budget cuts he had in mind, so rather than giving the committees the customary instructions telling them how much money they would have to cut, he wanted to show only the money they would have to spend.

This would have been quite a feat to achieve a few hours before committee consideration: The budget resolution consisted almost entirely of numbers, some of them thirteen digits long. "When is Newt going to ask us to do the numbers in Babylonian base sixty?" I asked a colleague, as we marveled at his impulsive ways. Nobody thought it beyond the realm of possibility for this mercurial temperament; his edicts were ever more outlandish and unpredictable. More substantively, he gutted the traditional committee system, reduced the power of committee chairmen, and centralized power in the Speaker's office. Bills reported out of a committee would mysteriously disappear and reappear rewritten. Gingrich, in his own flattering self-estimation, had become something of a prime minister, with powers comparable to those of the president.

After a year or so of Trotsky-style permanent revolution, his act began to wear thin. The government shutdown and the attempted coup against his speakership that followed weakened him.

Later, when he pushed ahead to impeach President Clinton, he ran into a buzz saw. Gingrich stepped down in the comic aftermath of the impeachment caper, and many Republicans breathed a sigh of relief.

His replacement as Speaker, Dennis Hastert, was a relatively innocuous vacuum, but Gingrich had made sweeping and irrevocable changes to the basic operation of the House. He had also effectively transformed the broader political culture. The presidential impeachment he engineered had unleashed an extraordinary, vitriolic polarization in the electorate. That the Dreyfus case of the 1990s should have been a bedroom farce was a testament to the power of culture war diversions to inflame passions and intensify divisions.

In any case, Newt's feral instinct and scorched-earth tactics lived on in the House whip and later majority leader Tom DeLay, who learned to throw his voice so that it issued from Hastert's lips. Under DeLay, also known as "the hammer," the same take-no-prisoners tactics continued until his own dethronement in late 2005 over a shady campaign finance scandal. Under DeLay, "pay for play"—the extortion of campaign funds from companies bidding for federal contracts or seeking favorable tax treatment—reached a crescendo. This was the period just before superlobbyist Jack Abramoff's arrest and imprisonment. Before his fall Abramoff made $20 million a year securing congressional favors for his clients—not least from Tom DeLay, whose staffers Abramoff hired into his lobbying firm.

The good times kept rolling through the golden years of the Bush administration, when the reflexive patriotism triggered by September 11 played to their advantage, until the Republicans hit a wall in 2006, when they lost both houses in the midterm elections. Now that the GOP was in the minority, it had little recourse in the

House, which in any case was a majoritarian body. (During their twelve years in control the Republicans had altered House rules to increase majority power beyond the already substantial level that had been the norm.)

At this point, the action shifted to the Senate. Now that the GOP was the minority party, it could avail itself of the peculiar rules and customs of the legislative chamber that vaunts itself as the world's greatest deliberate body. Despite our foreign policy elite's constant invocation of democracy as the highest ideal, America itself is not exactly a majoritarian democracy. Nowhere is that observation more in evidence than in the Senate, where the minority can prevent the majority from ruling, or even from bringing legislation to the floor.

Supreme Court justice Antonin Scalia has opined that the Senate is intentionally designed for gridlock.[2] In reality, the Constitution has relatively few provisions dealing with the Senate, and those that exist have mainly to do with member qualification, how the Senate is formed, and similar matters. The Constitution establishes vote thresholds in a few instances (ratification of treaties, for instance), but nowhere will one find the term "filibuster" or the basis for the belief that a sixty-vote threshold should be necessary for any legislative business. The Constitution merely states that the Senate, like the House (unless otherwise specified), shall make its own rules. And what rules it has made! The filibuster is a Senate rule, not a constitutional mandate. The current sixty-vote threshold is another one, which only dates back to 1975.

While it is true that founders like James Madison attempted to fashion a system to resist tyrannical accretions of power, they formulated their ideas, as did so many eighteenth-century political theorists, by analogy to the Newtonian laws that so impressed learned people of the Enlightenment. Just as the universe was a clockwork mechanism functioning in harmony and balance, so should a system of republican governance, so far as it was practically possible to fit that template. Although the Founding Fathers had different opinions about the primacy of the central government, they certainly did not want a *liberum veto* system similar to the one that was then in place in contemporary Poland, where one delegate to the Polish Diet could prevent its functioning. The resulting gridlock that Scalia so admires contributed to Poland's inability to defend its own national existence.

But however much the Founders were influenced by Enlightenment theory, they also grappled with the exigencies of the specific conditions and interests of thirteen culturally disparate former colonies. Contrary to Scalia's picture of the Senate as an institution designed in a Platonic vacuum, the actual institution comes to us with some less savory historical baggage attached. The restrictive, minoritarian makeup and procedures of the Senate enumerated in the Constitution (most were established piecemeal at later times) did not arise solely from a disinterested desire to create a bulwark against a hypothetical future tyrant. They came into being in the first place partly as a compromise to protect slave-holding interests in the less populous southern states, by balancing the population-determined House of Representatives. The history of the Senate for the next seven decades after the founding was closely bound up with the antebellum South's defense of slavery. After the Civil War, and for the next hundred years, the Senate was often the last ditch of defense for the Jim Crow system. The current sixty-vote filibuster threshold is a reduction from the previous sixty-seven-vote requirement, and was to some extent a reaction to the bitter fights Strom Thurmond and his segregationist colleagues waged through the mid-1960s against civil rights legislation. Thus, for the first 175 years of its history, the Senate's makeup and procedures assisted in the defense of slavery and segregation, with considerable success.

In recent years the Senate minority has been the ideal venue for the GOP. The Republican Party is no longer a party of governance, because it has no positive, workable agenda with which to exercise power: It has become the "anti" party par excellence. When it gains the majority in the House of Representatives, as it did in 2010, its style is so transparently primitive that it tends to alienate more voters than it attracts. But in the Senate, with its outwardly genteel procedural rigmarole, Republican politicians can hide behind institutional formalities while pursuing a strategy that consists almost entirely of negative campaigning rather than of co-governance. If one's goal is to obstruct, the Senate offers a nearly infinite variety of procedural levers with which to do so. And the result will generally be presented as "The Senate Fails to Pass . . ." rather than "The Senate GOP Obstructs . . ." by the media.

Obama had barely begun his term in office in early 2009, when Mitch McConnell, the Senate Republican leader, declared that his greatest legislative priority was . . . what? Jobs for Americans? Rescuing the financial system? Solving the housing collapse? No, none of those. His top priority was to ensure that Obama would be a one-term president. By his own admission Senator McConnell hated Obama more than he wanted to pull the country out of a deep crisis.*

The GOP's agenda is reflected in its recent embrace of the filibuster. Until 1970, filibusters were relatively rare, never exceeding single digits during the period of a two-year Congress. Their fre-

---

* But during the debt-ceiling negotiations the media began hailing McConnell as "the adult in the room," presumably because he was less theatrically extreme than the Tea Party freshmen.

quency steadily rose over the years, until the number in each Congress rose to the mid-to-high double digits in the early years of the Bush administration. But when the Republicans entered the minority in 2007, the number of filibusters more than doubled, to 139 during the 2007–2009 Congress. The fact that more than half of these filibusters were overcome suggests not that they were futile but that the time expended overcoming them was the whole point of the exercise.

Republicans are now operating on the Leninist principle of "the worse, the better." According to this principle, if they hold fast against every one of the administration's attempts at restarting the economy, the presidency and both houses of Congress will fall into their laps in 2012. I am not alone in ascribing nihilistic and destructive motives to the former party of Lincoln. Bruce Bartlett, who served as an economist in the Reagan administration, tried to explain our predicament in the fall of 2011.

> Basically, we're still stuck in the situation we were in three years ago, and we haven't made any progress at all, except that our problems are much worse because of political reasons, because we now have a crazy party in charge of one of the houses of our Congress, and they won't allow anything to happen, because it's in their vested interest to make things worse.[3]

Delay and gridlock have been the Republicans' principal objectives for the last three years, even as the country was fighting two wars and the economy was sliding off a cliff. They have so far been mostly successful in meeting their objectives. Undermining Americans' belief in their own institutions of self-government remains a prime GOP electoral strategy. But if delay and gridlock fall short of producing Karl Rove's dream of thirty years of unchallengeable one-party rule, there are other, even less democratic, techniques to fall back on. Ever since Republicans won majorities in a number of state legislatures in November 2010, they have systematically attempted to make it more difficult to vote, with onerous voter ID requirements (in Wisconsin, Republicans have legislated photo IDs while shutting DMV offices in areas where Democratic constituencies live and lengthening their hours of operation in GOP-dominated ones); narrower registration periods; residency requirements that may disenfranchise university students; shutdowns of early voting; and the repeal of same-day registration.

This legislative assault is moving America in a direction diametrically opposed to the arrow of progress that has governed the last two hundred years of its history, which has been pointed toward more political participation by more citizens. At one point in 2009 the so-called Tea Party movement (which claims to be independent but overwhelmingly supports GOP candidates) even flirted briefly with the concept of repealing the Seventeenth Amendment, which provides for the popular election of senators. Republicans never tire of self-righteously lecturing other countries about the wonders of democracy; exporting democracy (at the barrel of a gun) was a signature policy of the Bush administration. But domestically they don't want *those people* voting. Those people are anyone not likely to vote Republican. As Sarah Palin would say, they are not Real Americans, and by that she means anyone who doesn't look, think, or talk like the GOP base.

Politics ain't beanbag, to be sure. But the present-day Republican Party shows less and less resemblance to one of the traditional parties in a healthy two-party system that places a premium on broad coalitions, compromise, and a nonideological worldview. When they are in power, whether in statehouses, Congress, or the

White House, Republicans are magnetically drawn to practice political overreach along with scorched-earth tactics, be it through vote suppression, the K Street Project to force lobbying firms to hire only Republicans, or outing a covert CIA agent in their own administration to settle political scores, as happened to Valerie Plame. When they are out of power they focus single-mindedly on seizing up the wheels of government to prove to the American people that government just doesn't work—at least, when the GOP is out of power. These take-no-prisoners tactics flow naturally from an embittered, Manichaean mind-set. This mentality has grave implications for the health of our constitutional system. *Syncretic*

Dualism
good vs. evil

"*Non Idealogical World View*"

3

ALL WRAPPED UP IN
THE CONSTITUTION

Like biblical literalists, Republicans assert that the
Constitution is divinely inspired and inerrant. But also
like biblical literalists, they are strangely selective
about those portions of their favorite document that
they care to heed, and they favor rewriting it when it
stands in the way of their political agenda.

★ ★ ★

If you want total security, go to prison.
There you're fed, clothed, given medical care, and so on.
The only thing lacking ... is freedom.

—attributed to Dwight D. Eisenhower

One may be forgiven for finding it strange that people who
profess to revere the Constitution should so caustically
denigrate the institution that is supposed to be the material expression of its principles. The Republican tactic of inducing
public distrust of government is not only cynical, it is schizophrenic.
Which is not to say that all aspects of the federal government are
flawless, or that there should be no limit to its size or intrusiveness.

But while the size of the federal government has been a subject
of some deliberation recently, most Republican officeholders seem
oddly uninterested in government intrusiveness. Few voiced con-

cern about the effective repeal of Fourth Amendment protections against uncontrolled government surveillance, or of the weakening of habeas corpus and self-incrimination protections in the public hysteria following 9/11—or the fact that government-sanctioned torture emerged from the dark recesses of Dick Cheney's id to blot America's reputation worldwide. These unsavory developments would have horrified the Founding Fathers, but all Republicans, save for a few ineffectual dissenters, accepted them without a murmur. Should one object, they have a rote response: Boo! The terrorists will get you!

Whenever a momentary GOP hobbyhorse is *not* in the Constitution, however, Republicans of late have wanted to tinker with that supposedly perfect document. Recent years have seen constitutional amendment proposals for bans on flag burning and abortion; a federal definition of marriage (whatever happened to states' rights?); and a balanced budget (so much for countercyclical fiscal policy, or Alexander Hamilton's notions of a funded public debt). A wholesale revision of the Fourteenth Amendment definition of citizenship has also been suggested. Whatever crackpot scheme polls well with the "base," some Republican politician is bound to try to shoehorn into the Constitution.

It is said that only the Mormons believe that the Constitution is divinely inspired. But many partisan Republican voters, whether they call themselves libertarians or social conservatives, approach it with an attitude of near religious idolatry. It is an uninformed idolatry, which would seem paradoxical except that such behavior can routinely be found in all facets of life. Uncritical veneration, whether the object is a human being, an idea, or an inanimate object, leads to inaccurate judgments and doublethink. When combined with ignorance about the object in question, that veneration can lead to all manner of folly. The satirical paper *The Onion* published a piece whose headline says it all: "Area Man Passionate Defender of What He Imagines Constitution to Be."

The Framers did an excellent job of drawing up our charter of government. In the context of the time, when almost all European states were either despotic monarchies or oligarchies like the Republic of Venice, the Constitution was well-nigh miraculous. But it was hardly perfect, because it was written by fallible human beings—however enlightened—under the stress of hard circumstances and historical legacies, not all of them exemplary.

To start with, one might think that section 2 of Article I, the line about "the whole Number of free Persons, including those bound to Service for a Term of Years, and excluding Indians not taxed, three fifths of all other Persons," might give one pause to wonder about the changeless perfection of the Constitution, let alone its divine inspiration. Indentured servitude and chattel slavery would hardly seem to be features of the harmonious earthly paradise that the people who now go to town hall meetings in tricornered hats want to project back onto American society two and a quarter centuries ago. In those days only property owners were allowed to vote in most states, and some nonindentured whites lived in conditions that looked a lot like European serfdom: For example, the patroon system in New York State's Hudson Valley, under which wealthy oligarchs such as the Rensselaer family extracted feudal rents from their tenants, lasted until the mid-1840s. And it would be entertaining to see religious fundamentalists who dream of having no wall of separation between church and state subject themselves to the religious doctrines and taxes of the then newly constituted states that had established churches, such as Connecticut and Massachusetts (the latter's state-sanctioned church was not disestablished until 1833).

Strict construction of the Constitution is a delusion, like all forms of extreme textual interpretation, whether biblical literalism or literary deconstructionism. Old Testament verses about smiting one's foes (or exterminating whole peoples) stand in contradiction to those forbidding killing. Likewise with the Constitution: Is the constitutional right of free speech unconditional, or does it contradict the same document's promise "to ensure domestic tranquility" when that speech would levy insurrection against the government? How do we square the Tenth Amendment's grant of sovereignty to the states with the commerce clause? There are dozens of contradictions like these, and no document can be so comprehensive as to resolve them all, especially when we find ourselves having to legislate in circumstances undreamed of by the Framers.

The only way to manage them is by comity, reason, and a sense of proportion—in other words, with a sound judicial temperament. The Constitution is not a tablet hauled down from Mount Sinai but a charter of government drawn up in specific, urgent circumstances because the previous charter, the Articles of Confederation, was a failure. But for present-day Republicans, and even more for the Tea Party activists who run around in colonial garb, the Constitution is the most sacred document they have never read.

With respect to the First Amendment, almost everyone across the political spectrum is a hypocrite to some degree. We can all think of cases when we have wanted an ironclad and expansive interpretation of it to protect behavior we approve of and a narrow and exclusive reading to restrict behavior we disapprove of. But those who treat the Constitution as an inerrant text seem to have more problems than others. Money is speech, according to their view, and unlimited campaign contributions are an unfettered right for which our forefathers threw out the British tyrants. Flag burning, on the other hand, is not free expression, because they don't like it. (There is an additional irony here: The flag is a secular symbol, so to refer to burning the flag as a "desecration," as flag amendment proponents habitually do, applies sacred language to a secular symbol, reflecting the sort of idol worship that the Bible explicitly forbids.) When opponents of a Republican administration dare to make statements critical of government policy in times of war, the faithful will accuse them of "giving aid and comfort to the enemy." But when the governor of a southern state talks about secession from the United States in response to a federal government policy he doesn't like, there is no mention of treason.

This sort of one-sidedness is rooted in a mind-set that bears resemblance, ironically enough, to Vladimir Lenin's basic precept of politics: *kto-kogo*, literally "who-whom," meaning who does what to whom. Lenin believed that revolutionary violence committed by the vanguard of the proletariat (a group conveniently defined by him alone) was perfectly legitimate. Violence committed against the vanguard of the proletariat, on the other hand, was illegitimate. We all practice in-group favoritism in everyday life, and in our ideological preferences, but most of us make a conscious effort not to let it degenerate into chronic doublethink. And as for constitutions and legal statutes, their whole purpose is to apply consistent rules and to restrain such irrational favoritism.

Perhaps the only amendment to the Constitution that people who self-identify as Republicans believe to be absolute, unfettered, and unlimited is the second one, which guarantees the right to bear arms. I, too, believe in the presumptive right of a law-abiding adult to own a firearm, and have exercised that right. But I am not persuaded that this right should extend to felons, minors, the mentally ill, or persons under a restraining order. Again, a rule of reason applies. One would also think that it might not be wise to extend the unrestricted right to purchase firearms to terrorist suspects or drug runners. But crackpot legal theorists on the right, who have no problem when it comes to distinctly unconstitutional restrictions on rights of privacy or habeas corpus, not to mention the right to a speedy trial, to have evidence openly presented, even the right not to be tortured (all enumerated in the Bill of Rights), suddenly become unrelenting constitutional absolutists when it comes to the purchase of firearms. Why? In situations such as this, when behavior defies all rational explanation, it is generally helpful to look at the money trail.

At the same time that the Bush administration was telling us to be afraid, be very afraid, of terrorists, Attorney General John Ashcroft was fighting for the prerogative to destroy gun purchase records.[1] Had he done otherwise, he and the Bush administration would have fallen afoul of the National Rifle Association (NRA), and its political contributions might have dried up. Likewise, the straw purchases* of automatic weapons for Mexican drug cartels were protected by the "conservative" faithful in Congress who ostensibly hate illegal drugs and illegal Mexicans almost as much as they hate a disappointing haul from their latest fund-raising event. When ill-conceived sting operations set up by both the Bush and Obama administrations came to light (the Drug Enforcement Administration allowed guns to get into the hands of the cartels, ostensibly to track their movements), a House committee chaired by Republican Darrell Issa bore down on the case like Bulldog Drummond. But Issa testily forbade any mention of the flawed legal process that had permitted gunrunners for the cartels to purchase the assault rifles in question in the first place.[2] His lack of curiosity was not a sign of congenital stupidity, because most members of Congress possess a high measure of low cunning—if it were otherwise,

---

* The purchase of a firearm by one person on behalf of another person who may not have the legal right to purchase a firearm.

they would never be elected. Rather, it stemmed from an all-consuming fear of the NRA, and of how that lobby can distort facts into the corrosive charge of being "antigun." NRA propaganda is nearly as powerful an incentive as NRA contributions.

What sensitized me to this matter was less the bare facts of the case than the sheer emotional callousness of the gun lobby after the 2007 Virginia Tech shootings, when thirty-two students and faculty members were murdered. A group of belligerent activists showed up on the scene within days of the shooting, vehemently arguing that all students and faculty ought to have the right to carry a concealed firearm in the classroom. Whatever the validity of the arguments for or against this particular policy, the decision to descend on the campus to make a controversial and divisive proposal while parents were still grieving over their children amply displays the monomania and lack of empathy of gun-lobby ideologues.

When they won a majority of state legislatures in 2010, Republican politicians promptly attempted to put their idée fixe about the Second Amendment into states' statutes. Concealed carry in a bar? No problem! Concealed carry at a packed football stadium? What could possibly go wrong there? The Florida legislature passed, and Governor Rick Scott signed into law, a bill that would prohibit physicians from even *asking* patients (for example, ones exhibiting suicidal symptoms) if they owned a firearm.[3] The draft bill would have levied fines of up to $5 million and jail time for any physician who violated it, although these draconian punishments were reduced before passage. So much for the GOP's claim, loudly enunciated during the debate over the health care bill, that the government shouldn't come between patients and their doctors. The issue, of course, had nothing whatsoever to do with the legal right of a citizen to own a firearm. The Florida legislature was grandstanding on behalf of the NRA.

Is there a constitutional right for law-abiding citizens to possess firearms? Yes, there is. But it is revealing of the psychological insecurities and revenge fantasies of a large, politically active segment of the population that it should devote so much energy and passion not only to maintaining the right to possess lethal weaponry, but to expanding this prerogative in marginal or even plainly ridiculous circumstances. All this fuss over a provision that makes up less than one half of 1 percent of all of the words in the Constitution is rather puzzling. It is a pity these people do not seem to care quite so passionately about the remaining 99.5 percent.

The Third Amendment, which prevents soldiers from setting up shop in people's homes without their consent, doesn't get nearly as much attention. But with the Fourth Amendment, which protects people from warrantless search and seizure, the conservative who defends the Second Amendment to the last breath is back to Leninist who-whom thinking. For all the supposed belief in the primacy and autonomy of the individual against the state espoused by the followers of Ayn Rand, and for all the "don't tread on me" sloganeering of the Tea Party, both groups have been remarkably supine in the face of recent actions by the executive branch that have effectively rendered the Fourth Amendment null and void. The "live free or die" mantra popular among self-styled conservatives is only a self-flattering pose, effectively negated by the authoritarian national security and law and order mentality that has gripped the Republican faithful. Believing that they are the most patriotic Americans, and that they have nothing to fear, they rationalize warrantless surveillance as something the government will only use against terrorists, foreigners, criminally inclined minorities, and other evildoers.

In their indifference to the constitutional right to privacy, Republicans are, alas, on firm political if not constitutional ground.

One might think Democrats would oppose the erosion of the constitutional right to privacy, as well as all the other encroachments on civil liberties inflicted on Americans in recent years, if only on a purely opportunistic basis, even if principle alone did not incline them to do so. After all, if George Bush was *for* warrantless surveillance, Democrats must be *against* it. Accordingly, they could presumably have rallied all the voters who opposed Bush and his executive overreach by means of a polarizing issue, right? Think again. I knew the game was up in the summer of 2008 just before the Democratic convention when Candidate Obama, with all eyes upon him prior to his coronation in Denver, voted to indemnify telecommunications corporations against any claims arising from their participation in a program of unconstitutional surveillance. Since his inauguration Obama has institutionalized, and even expanded, many of the illegal measures Bush first conceived in the aftermath of the terrorist attacks.

And so it is with the Fifth, Sixth, and Eighth amendments. If George Bush took the pioneering role of engineering detentions without charge, undermining due process, forbidding the defendant to see the evidence against him, torturing, and so on, Barack Obama did nothing to reverse these measures. In so doing he made these infractions part of a corpus of secret administrative law neither accessible to nor challengeable by ordinary citizens. Our last two presidents have laid the foundation on which all police states rest.

Our present government would be less of an insulting farce if either of the two ruling parties had the honesty to propose an outright repeal of the Bill of Rights, for it is a virtual dead letter. Sad as it is to say, there would be no significant movement to prevent them from doing so. Civil liberties lawyers may cringe at that statement, but I believe the constant invocation of terrorism has so conditioned the public into a state of "wholesome fear," as storm trooper leader Ernst Röhm liked to call it, that their constitutional rights mean nothing to millions of people, perhaps even a voting majority. Americans for the most part, as unattractive as the idea is, do not care very much about their rights, above all what may be the most precious right of all: what former Supreme Court justice Louis D. Brandeis called "the right to be let alone—the most comprehensive of the rights and the right most valued by civilized men." The elderly, who tend to be the most fearful and cautious age group, have in general let their exaggerated concerns about terrorism (statistically a lesser probability than a senior drowning in his bathtub) override whatever traditional concerns they might once have had about privacy. And for the young, who are growing up with Facebook and with surveillance cameras in their high schools and school buses, personal privacy, and indeed any real sense of the traditional distinction between the public and private realms, may be a meaningless abstraction.

The Republican Party has engaged in a full-scale assault on what it calls "judicial activism" (meaning judicial independence). Newt Gingrich went on a tirade about this in Iowa in December 2011, stating that if elected president he would ignore judicial decisions he didn't like—an extreme example of a widespread attitude. The party's belief that national security *as it defines it* should trump the most fundamental rights laid down by the Framers bears a heavy burden for the evisceration of the Constitution it claims to revere. Madison and the Founders were very clear on this point: that constitutional republics should not be armed camps. The GOP's version of national security—perpetual war, a bloated military budget, and diminished constitutional protections—is a far cry from anything the Founding Fathers would recognize or advocate.

Democrats—ever sensitive to the whiff of corporate money (as in their vote to indemnify the telecommunications companies for illegal surveillance), or afraid of being tarred as soft on terrorism, soft on crime, or soft in general—have closely followed the GOP's trail. None of this would have happened in the presence of a vigilant press or a resolute citizenry conscious of its rights and skeptical of distractions, scare tactics, or intimidation. Sadly, we have been dumbed down, beaten down, and conditioned into accepting the invalidation of the Constitution as the new norm with scarcely a whimper. A public that pays more attention to reality TV than its status as free citizens cannot withstand an unremitting encroachment on its liberties by calculating, unscrupulous, and power-hungry leaders. The crowning tragedy—or sick joke—is that those who have postured and preened the most ostentatiously about their devotion to the Constitution have been the most indifferent to its destruction.

For destruction it is. There are now numerous provisions in the Bill of Rights that exist on paper just as the Estates-General did during the French monarchy—it existed on paper but was moribund. If a free citizenry is too apathetic, too intimidated, too distracted, or just plain too ignorant to exercise its statutory liberties, those liberties will not last long.

4

A DEVIL'S DICTIONARY

How Republicans have mastered the art of communicating with ordinary people in their own vernacular, while Democrats remain tone-deaf and tongue-tied.

☆ ☆ ☆

Polonius: "What do you read, my lord?"
Hamlet: "Words, words, words."

—*Hamlet*, Act 2, Scene 2

How did Republicans manage to seize control of the way Americans speak about public life? Democrats do not understand the power of language. Their initiatives are posed in impenetrable policy-speak: the Patient Protection and Affordable Care Act. The *what*? Can anyone even remember that? No wonder the pejorative "Obamacare" won out. Contrast that with the Republicans' USA PATRIOT Act (the Uniting and Strengthening America by Providing Appropriate Tools Required to Intercept and Obstruct Terrorism Act). You're a patriot, aren't you? Who would dare be against that? Most Americans do not have a college education. Do the Democrats really expect them to have a clear understanding of what a stimulus bill is supposed to do? Why didn't the White House just call it the jobs bill and keep pounding on that theme? Obama has taken a drubbing for failing to focus on jobs, but his real mistake was not hiring more advertising types to come up with catchier names for his bills.

You know that Social Security and Medicare are in jeopardy when even Democrats refer to them as "entitlements." Entitlement has a negative sound: Somebody who says he's entitled selfishly claims something he doesn't deserve. Why not call them "earned benefits"—which is what they are, because we all contribute payroll taxes to fund them? It would never occur to a Democrat. Republicans don't make that mistake; they are relentlessly on message: There is no "estate tax"—it is the "death tax." Heaven forbid that the Walton family should have to give up one penny of its $86 billion fortune when the paterfamilias dies.

Capturing the terms of the debate through the adroit use of language has allowed the GOP to bamboozle millions of people about their own material interests. It was not always thus. You would have been hard-pressed to find an uneducated farmer during the depression of the 1890s who did not have a very accurate idea about exactly who and what was shafting him. An unemployed worker in a bread line in 1932 would have felt little gratitude to the Rockefellers or the Mellons. But that is not the case in the present economic crisis. After a riot of unbridled greed such as the world has not seen since the conquistadores' looting expeditions, after an unprecedentedly broad and rapid transfer of wealth upward by Wall Street and its corporate satellites, where has popular anger been directed? If the media are to be believed, for most of the last three and a half years the public has been incensed about "Washington spending"—which has increased mostly to provide unemployment compensation, food stamps, and Medicaid to those economically damaged by the previous decade's corporate saturnalia. Any residual anger is harmlessly diverted to pseudoissues: death panels, gay marriage, abortion, and so on.

It may seem frivolous to harp on such an abstract matter as

language at a time when we face war, a $15 trillion national debt, and a shrinking middle class. But words are the vehicles that convey political ideas, so we had better pay attention to them. There is a common misconception that language arises more or less organically, and that people use whichever word or phrase pops into their heads, much like a bird building its nest with the random twigs it sees on the ground. But in public life, political operatives have painstakingly chosen words to help shape voters' acceptance or rejection of an idea even before they have made a conscious effort to think about it.

I became aware of the overwhelming role of language in contemporary politics shortly before the 9/11 attacks. At that time, the word "homeland" was practically unused in the American vernacular. It had a slightly archaic sound to it, and was invoked generally only as a stilted translation of the German *heimat*, or as a euphemism for the bantustans created by South Africa's apartheid government in its policy to rid itself of the native population.

But strangely enough, in the summer of 2001 a newly published RAND Corporation study found its way into my congressional office in-box: *Preparing the U.S. Army for Homeland Security*. Even then it struck me as odd that someone would use that word, despite the penchant of the military-industrial complex—of which the RAND Corporation is a cog—for coining new buzzwords. Around that same time, the congressionally mandated U.S. Commission on National Security/21st Century (the so-called Hart-Rudman Commission) had issued its final report, which contained a chapter with the pretentious title "Securing the National Homeland." It is possible that the savvy bureaucrats at RAND adopted the commission's buzzword in their book's title to get in step with the evolving zeitgeist. But "homeland" was still a term no American would have used colloquially when referring to his country.

A couple of months later it was as if someone had flipped a switch: Suddenly everybody—politicians, the media, all the opinion shapers who inhabit the American landscape—was incessantly using the word "homeland" and giving no indication that it was any sort of novelty, much less that someone was conditioning them to use it. Even the normally inarticulate George W. Bush flawlessly recited his lines—lines which often included a reference to the homeland or homeland security.

Some unsung bureaucrat, or a functionary at one of the government-dependent think tanks, had clearly done his linguistic research. If the Bush administration had gone ahead and created a U.S. Department of Domestic Security it would have sounded like the interior ministry of a minor Warsaw Pact satellite state. Besides, domestic has other meanings, including the dreaded (by Republicans) "domestic partnership." The U.S. Department of Internal Defense would have been too cumbersome, and besides, what was the old Department of Defense supposed to be doing? "Homeland Security" was perfect: old-fashioned, vaguely patriotic, and unsullied by any connotation that 95 percent of Americans would be aware of. As for the remaining 5 percent, were they with us or against us?*

The linguistic offensive kicked into high gear after September 2001. Amid such cheery tidings as the self-satisfied pronouncement, by an anonymous government official, that America would be engaged in the "next Hundred Years' War,"[1] or Secretary of State Condoleezza Rice's slightly less ambitious declaration of a thirty-year "generational struggle," the Global War on Terrorism debuted to rave reviews.

---

* There is poetic justice in the fact that the new headquarters complex for the Department of Homeland Security is being constructed on the site of an abandoned mental hospital.

The war on terrorism was a propagandistic success just as surely as it was a failure both of logic and of national strategy. Nations have declared wars against other nations since time immemorial. Now, for the first time, we were declaring war on a tactic. Did this mean that the United States would be at war with the Tamil Tigers, Chechen rebels, or the Maoist guerrillas in India's West Bengal province? Presumably not, but the label was sufficiently broad that the president and his advisers could intervene anywhere militarily at will, and for an indefinite period, pursuant to the absurdly broad Authorization of Use of Military Force resolution that was rushed through a panicked and supine Congress in September 2001.

In military terms, the war on terrorism failed just as our domestic crusades symbolically styled as "wars" have failed: the war on poverty, the war on drugs. But in public relations terms, which is what the American system of governing is increasingly about—not solving problems, but shaping perceptions through the adroit use of rousing or soothing phrases—it was a smash hit. It induced courtier media personalities like Thomas Friedman to swoon over the righteousness of it all—and, more important, they swooned over the nominal author of the crusade, George W. Bush, who, as the undistinguished offspring of an elite political family, had lucked into the presidency after a disputed election.

Like an antibiotic-resistant bacterium, the war on terrorism soon mutated into something else: the war on "terror." This subtle but telling semantic shift was yet another turn of the screw. Terrorism is at least a technique of militants. Terror is an emotion. How can one make war on a subjective mental state? Yet "war on terror" has now become the shorthand label of choice of government, media, and popular speech when describing the overseas adventures that are bankrupting us.

My sentiments

In his 1946 essay "Politics and the English Language," George Orwell concluded that the prevailing vagueness and ambiguity of political language was a symptom of the decadence of a culture. That may be the case: a rubric like "war on terror" illustrates our national inability to make basic categorical distinctions. But Orwell underestimated the emotional power of those words and phrases, despite their imprecision and the questions they beg. He seemed to think at that time that the verbal falsity he was describing was a by-product of sloppy thinking by stupid or careless ideologues. It was only two years later, in 1984, that he described a totalitarian society where attitudes were successfully bent and molded by the conscious efforts of political leaders to shape the language of thought. In that case, the distortion of public language was not inadvertent but deliberate.

"War on terror" is one of those phrases that conditioned us in the same manner that the proles of Orwell's Oceania were conditioned by Newspeak. Our rulers designated it as a war much as real wars like World War II. But traditional wars have a definable end and require sacrifices on the home front. So the Bush administration had to attempt to cast the war on terror as a war that demanded shared sacrifice, not as a grab for oil or a racket for defense contractors. Our sacrifices on the home front consisted of receiving a tax cut and obeying an exhortation to go shopping.

Part of the Republicans' success in this area is due to the proper use of "framing" techniques. This mainly entails using short, simple, easily understood words and phrases—positive words for what you are defending, negative words for what you are attacking. Orwell spelled it out sixty-five years ago: Use short Anglo-Saxon words with an evocative meaning and avoid fancy polysyllabic words and phrases that look as if they came from a Latin dictionary. Hence, jobs bill rather than stimulus bill.

The difference in the two parties' use of language originates in the different ways in which they generate their ideas. The source of many, if not most, Democratic policy ideas can be traced to academia: One has only to think of president of Princeton Woodrow Wilson, the New Deal's brain trust, Kennedy's best and brightest, or the Ivy League graduates who have clustered around Clinton and Obama. Their verbiage, like their thinking, has tended to be arcane, qualified, and convoluted.

Republican style can be traced back to about the same time, when Wilson was touting his political vision for a new world order, but it came from a different source. Early in the twentieth century the GOP began to borrow the techniques that their supporters in big business were developing to sell products: from the nascent trade of corporate advertising. It is no coincidence that two of the pioneers of American corporate advertising and public relations were men of decidedly reactionary impulses.

The first trailblazer was Ivy Lee. He is often considered the founder of modern public relations and the originator of corporate crisis communications.* In 1914 he went to work for the Rockefeller interests after coal miners striking at one of the mines they controlled in Ludlow, Colorado, were massacred by the National Guard. Between nineteen and twenty-five people were killed, including two women and eleven children. Lee's press releases claimed that their deaths were the result of an overturned camp stove. Ivy Lee was one of the first members of the Council on Foreign Relations when it was founded just after World War I; he was thus co-opted into America's foreign policy establishment. Shortly

---

* Lee is the ultimate inspiration for British Petroleum's heavy advertising of the Gulf of Mexico as an ideal vacation venue after the company despoiled it.

before he died in 1934, Congress began investigating his public relations work on behalf of the notorious German chemical monopoly I.G. Farben, which helped fund Hitler's rise to power and would later develop the poison gas used in the Nazi death camps.

The other pioneer of political public relations was Edward Bernays, a nephew of Sigmund Freud, who sharpened his skills writing prowar propaganda for the Committee on Public Information during World War I. After the war he decided that the word "propaganda" had a negative ring, due to its use by the defeated Germans; he came up with a new phrase, "public relations," which has a distinctly more Madison Avenue sound. In 1928, in his influential *Propaganda*, Bernays claimed that manipulating public opinion was a necessary part of democracy. According to his daughter, Bernays believed the common people were "not to be relied upon, [so] they had to be guided from above." She would later say that her father believed in "enlightened despotism"—a system through which intelligent men such as himself would keep the mob in line through the clever use of subliminal PR campaigns. His clients included not only such megacorporations as Procter & Gamble, the United Fruit Company, and the American Tobacco Company (through clever advertising campaigns, he sought to remove the traditional stigma against women smoking), but also Republican president Calvin Coolidge. Bernays did not feel it would be strategic to allay the public's fear of communism and urged his clients to play on popular emotions and magnify that fear. His work laid some of the foundation of the McCarthyite hysteria of the 1950s. *Life* magazine named Bernays one of the one hundred most influential Americans of the twentieth century.

It would take some time for Lee's and Bernays's pathbreaking work to percolate through the ranks of Republican discourse. But early signs can be seen in the Nixon presidency, when Vice President

Spiro Agnew appealed to the "silent majority" by sneering at an "effete corps of impudent snobs" who supposedly ruled America. Reagan, who was a natural performer, perfected the act and honed the speech patterns and disarming language that were geared to appeal to "ordinary Americans"—not so far off from Sarah Palin's real Americans. But Reagan radiated optimism, and his pose was more grandfatherly than adversarial. Despite his bedrock anticommunism, Reagan instinctively understood when it was time to negotiate with the Soviet leadership, despite the opposition of many of his advisers and movement conservatives throughout the country.

While there is a slavish cult around Reagan in the present-day Republican Party, the current GOP follows neither his basic political flexibility nor his rhetorical style. His messaging, while certainly more effective than his flat-footed opponents Carter and Mondale, was infused with cheerfulness rather than scolding, hope rather than impending doom. Reagan's rhetorical affect did not persist when he left office. A characteristic moment exemplifying the style that would succeed his occurred at the 1992 Republican convention in Houston, when Pat Buchanan fused all the elements of fear, loathing, and Manichaean ideology in his "culture wars" address. This style reached its full flower in the rhetorical techniques used by Newt Gingrich, who even sought to instruct his colleagues in the dark arts of verbal assault.

In 1990, Gingrich offered up a memo to Republican candidates titled "Language: A Key Mechanism of Control." This document was intended to be a primer on the use of language for Republicans running for office who needed to master political buzz phrases. As Gingrich modestly put it, it was for Republicans who said to themselves, "I wish I could speak like Newt." His advice was really quite straightforward. The former history teacher counseled neophytes to use optimistic or soothing words to describe their own political program and relentlessly disparaging words to criticize their opponent's agenda. The title in itself is revealing. Note that it does not suggest that language is a key mechanism of persuasion or influence. Control is what one does to laboratory rats or prisoners of a totalitarian state, not free citizens of a democracy. If you pay close attention to Newt's own language, clues about his character always pile up.[2]

Lee, Bernays, and Gingrich have all had a lasting impact on the political use of language in America. If you seek monuments to their accomplishments, you have to look no further than your daily paper or television news program. It is to them that we owe stories about "collateral damage" rather than "dead civilians." In that spirit, allow me to offer up my own devil's dictionary of contemporary American political terms.

> **American Exceptionalism:** a doctrine whose proponents hold that by divine dispensation America is exempt from all laws governing international norms, physics, or rationality.

> **authentic:** used to describe a candidate who is unaware of current events and doesn't read a newspaper, and is proud of it.

> **class warfare:** a technique by which teachers, nurses, firemen, and cashiers are believed to be oppressing derivatives traders and CEOs, which includes unreasonably complaining that their wages aren't keeping up with the cost of their health insurance.

> **conservative:** a person profoundly respectful of heritage, tradition, and old-fashioned values while preaching the revolution and strip-mining the Grand Canyon for high-sulfur coal.

> **Darwin's theory of evolution:** an evil doctrine that denies the teachings of the Bible. Social Darwinism, on the other hand, is

what made America great and is perfectly consistent with the Sermon on the Mount.

elites: insufferable, overeducated snobs who are not real Americans and may in fact be French. Mitt Romney (Harvard MBA and JD) and George W. Bush (Yale, Harvard) have often criticized such scoundrels.

empower: If an American worker loses his pension or Social Security, he is empowered.

free-market capitalism: the economic system by which Halliburton gets sole-source, cost-plus government contracts.

global warming: a hoax perpetrated by a worldwide conspiracy of biased scientists. Fortunately it is being combated by right-wing foundations, oil companies, televangelists, and other disinterested believers in objective fact.

job creators: the truly creative engines of economic growth in our society: real-estate flippers, mortgage-backed securities bundlers, leveraged buyout specialists, dividend drawers, and hedge-fund billionaires.

level playing field: what every lobbyist wants in the spirit of fairness. The only way to achieve it is by bribing politicians to award a sole-source contract to his client.

liberal (pronounced *librull*): a satanic ideologue who is at once a socialist leveler, an elitist defender of privilege, an atheist, and a secret Muslim determined to bring sharia law to America.

patriot: someone who loves America more than he loves the majority of the people living therein.

populist: an advocate for the interests of "real" Americans who vehemently fights for the abolition of all government regulation of Wall Street investment banks.

prolife: the unconditional support of the first nine months of a human being's existence. After that period has expired, the same human being has an unconditional right to be executed by the state, sent off to war, or die without health insurance.

real Americans: the minority of Americans who look, think, and act exactly as I do.

rogue state: a country that violates international law by committing armed aggression, torturing prisoners, assassinating opponents, and possessing weapons of mass destruction. cf: **American Exceptionalism**

sharia law: a fundamentalist religious doctrine imposed on a given political jurisdiction. Any resemblance to public statutes on abortion in the Commonwealth of Virginia is purely coincidental.

take our country back: Give us what we want right now, even if we don't know what it is.

Tea Party: people covered by Medicare who hate socialized medicine.

Washington spending: the bad sort of spending that doesn't go toward earmarks to campaign contributors, subsidies to big oil, or the military's half-trillion-dollar budget. Everyone knows the Pentagon is across the Potomac in Virginia, not in Washington.

win-win situation: see **level playing field**.

5

TAXES AND THE RICH

**The GOP cares, over and above every other item
on its political agenda, about the rich contributors
who keep them in office. This is why tax increases
on the wealthy have become an absolute Republican
taboo. Caught between their own rich contributors
and their voters, Democrats are conflicted
and compromised.**

★ ★ ★

"The very rich are different from you and me...."
Yes, they have more money.

—Ernest Hemingway, taking a pot shot at F. Scott Fitzgerald
in the original version of "The Snows of Kilimanjaro"

lthough you won't find it in their party platform, the GOP's
mission is to protect and further enrich America's plutocracy. The party's caterwauling about deficits and debt is so
much eyewash to blind the public. In reality, Republicans act as
bellhops for corporate America and the superrich behind those
corporations. In the calculus of Washington politics as practiced by
the GOP, wealthy individuals and corporations are interchange-
able: Mitt Romney may have said more than he knew when he
pleaded that "corporations are people!" They are indeed people, a
very select group of people in executive suites and boardrooms who

draw a wildly disproportionate share of the benefits from the tax code—a tax code that the GOP has manipulated relentlessly to produce exactly that outcome.* As for the rest of us, Republicans have of late been strangely indifferent; some GOP presidential candidates have even offered proposals that would increase taxes on people of modest means. One might think Republicans would be enthusiastic about extending their tax-cut agenda to low-income earners paying regressive rates on their payroll taxes. These folks, who struggle from paycheck to paycheck just to keep their heads above water, would benefit the most from tax relief. But the GOP has been uncharacteristically hesitant when it comes to tax cuts for the ordinary Americans they claim to champion.

Whatever else President Obama has accomplished, his $4 trillion deficit reduction offer during the debt-ceiling crisis in the summer of 2011 did perform the useful service of smoking out Republican hypocrisy. The GOP refused to accept the offer because it could not abide so much as a one-tenth of 1 percent increase on the tax rates of the Walton family or the Koch brothers, much less a repeal of the carried interest rule that permits billionaire hedge fund managers to pay income tax at a lower effective rate than cops or nurses. Republicans finally settled on a deal that had far less deficit reduction—and even fewer spending cuts!—than Obama's proposal, because of their iron resolution to protect our society's overclass at all costs.

The GOP's indulgence of its campaign contributors is perhaps the single most outstanding characteristic of the party, although their rivals on the other side of the aisle are also well versed in the

---

* Corporations are persons? Really? Do corporations register for the draft at age eighteen? Are they called for jury duty? Legal sophistry must yield to common sense.

practice of buck raking. To give one small but illuminating example: On November 17, 2011, the House passed by a margin of 298 to 121 a measure that would define pizza as a vegetable for the purposes of the school lunch program. To quote a Reuters news article:

> "It's an important victory," said Corey Henry, spokesman for the American Frozen Food Institute (AFFI). That trade association lobbied Congress on behalf of frozen pizza sellers like ConAgra Foods Inc. and Schwan Food Co. and French fry makers McCain Foods Ltd. and J.R. Simplot Co., the latter best known as a supplier to fast-food company McDonald's Corp.[1]

During 2010, ConAgra gave $154,200 in political contributions and spent $400,000 on lobbying.[2] Granted that the average American can spare zero dollars to contribute to politicians or to lobby Congress, $154,200 divided among 535 representatives and senators comes to $288 per elected official. (In 2006, the last year that party breakouts are available, ConAgra gave 16 percent to Democrats and 84 percent to Republicans.[3]) What is noteworthy about the $288 is not how much money in aggregate washes through our political system, but how cheaply you can buy a politician.

Republicans have attempted to camouflage their solicitude for the wealthy and corporations with a fog of misleading rhetoric. John Boehner is fond of saying, "We won't raise *anyone's* taxes," as if the take-home pay of an Olive Garden waitress were inextricably bound up with whether Warren Buffett pays his capital gains as ordinary income or at a lower rate. Another chestnut is that millionaires and billionaires are "job creators." U.S. corporations have recently had their most profitable quarters in history; at the end of

2011, Apple was sitting on $97.6 billion in cash, more than the GDP of most small countries. So where are the jobs? Overwhelmingly, they went to China.[4]

Another smokescreen is the "small business" meme, since standing up for Mom and Pop's corner store is politically more attractive than shilling for a megacorporation. Raising taxes on the wealthy will kill the ability of small businesses to hire; that is the GOP lament every time some Democrat offers an amendment to increase taxes on incomes over $1 million. But the number of small businesses with an annual net taxable income over a million dollars is de minimis, if they exist at all, as they would no longer constitute small businesses. And as data from the nonpartisan Center for Economic and Policy Research have shown, small businesses account for only 7.2 percent of total employment in the United States, a significantly smaller share of total employment than in most countries of the Organization for Economic Cooperation and Development (OECD), which includes the United States, Canada, Australia, Japan, and Chile, in addition to most European countries.[5]

The GOP's inflated rhetoric about protecting small business occasionally reaches such comic levels that one is hard-pressed to distinguish it from satire. In September 2011, House Republicans issued a report condemning the supposedly job-killing regulations of the Obama administration. The administration had proposed a rule to restrict the trade in Burmese pythons, a huge, highly dangerous, and invasive species of snake that has been devastating wildlife in the Everglades and, should it prove adaptable to colder climates, could spread northward as far as coastal Delaware. The Republicans concluded that banning a reptile that can swallow an alligator or a small child might "devastate a small but thriving sector of the economy" and that the rule "has significant implications

The Bene was passed

for small businesses across the United States."[6] Now that I think about it, I wonder whether the Republicans' pro-snake position is based on their economic philosophy, or whether it is professional courtesy toward reptiles.

The GOP's ritual exalting of small business is a subset of a larger narrative in Republican messaging: the appeal to popular nostalgia for a small-town America where real Americans live. The Mom and Pop store, the local hardware emporium, the barbershop where the owner knows your name—all fit into a gauzy mental picture of a small community where the sun always seems to be shining and neighbors help one another out. Those who shape the GOP message have carefully crafted it as a counterpoint to the contrasting image of the anonymous and menacing big cities of the two coasts, where foreigners make up an increasing share of the population and alien cosmopolite ideas rule.

Yet what have Republicans done when it comes to advancing economic policies that would assure the viability of the small-town America they claim to adore? Did they support changes in the tax code to help small business fight off chain retailers? Did they oppose trade bills that would jeopardize small- and medium-size manufacturers by exposing them to competition from starvation-wage manufacturers overseas? Did they oppose tax advantages that big companies can accrue through leveraged buyouts of competitors?* I see no evidence they lifted a finger.

On the contrary, Republican ideology celebrates outsourcing, globalization, and takeovers as the glorious fruits of capitalism's "creative destruction." I saw for myself how Republican propo-

---

* Companies can write off the debt they assume to finance a takeover of another company in order to raid its pension fund, strip its assets, and liquidate the company.

nents of globalized vulture capitalism, such as Grover Norquist, Dick Armey, Phil Gramm, and Lawrence Kudlow, extolled this process as an unalloyed benefit. They were quick to denounce as socialism any attempt to mitigate its impact on society. Yet their own ideology is nothing more than an upside-down utopianism, a nineteenth-century absolutist twin of Marxism. If millions of people's interests are damaged in the process, it is a necessary and inevitable outcome of scientific laws that must never be tampered with.

I recall that in the late 1990s, some prolabor congressmen wanted to correct serious labor abuses occurring in the Northern Mariana Islands, a Pacific commonwealth of the United States. The territory was exempt from U.S. wage and workplace safety laws, but it was permitted to send garments manufactured there to the United States free of tariffs, because they were defined by law as "made in USA." There were persistent reports of near-gulag labor conditions, including barbed wire around the factories to keep workers from leaving. Forced abortions were among the abuses reportedly taking place against female workers who became pregnant, based on the idea that there shouldn't be any useless mouths to feed in a free-trade zone. To keep its privileged status, the entrepreneurs in the islands hired superlobbyist Jack Abramoff to lobby the Hill. Abramoff's friend Tom DeLay ensured that the House never considered legislation to end the abuses in the Marianas, even though one bill had a majority of House members sponsoring it. Even the sanctimonious prolife claims of the GOP receded before the dominant principle animating the party: Nothing must ever get in the way of the rich getting richer, especially when they use lobbyists to hand out cash to obliging congressmen.

When I was growing up in Ohio, both the cities and small towns had a profusion of small- to medium-size manufacturing businesses: tool-and-die works, sheet-metal fabricators, metal-casting companies, and parts suppliers for the larger industries, such as the car companies and the rubber industry. Now, thanks to this glorious creative destruction, most of them are gone—along with job security, a defined pension, and health benefits. But somebody made out pretty well in the conversion of the American economy from a diversified manufacturing colossus into a financial oligopoly. There was no one event, no single piece of legislation responsible for this transformation. But three decades of trade legislation to facilitate the offshoring of jobs, tax policies favoring looting over investment, and the deregulation of Wall Street's financial chicanery favored this transformation at every turn. And Republicans consistently favored those polices in their platform promoting free trade, tax relief, and deregulation.

Republicans have assiduously spread the myth that Americans are conspicuously overtaxed. But compared to other OECD countries, the effective rates of U.S. taxation are among the lowest. Among the thirty-three developed countries of the OECD, America's taxes are the fourth lowest; only those of Turkey, Mexico, and Chile are lower.[7] Lately the GOP has taken up the mantra that the top corporate income tax rate of 35 percent is confiscatory Bolshevism. But again, the effective rate is much lower. Did GE pay 35 percent in 2010 on its net profits of $14 billion? No. It paid zero.*

When pressed, Republicans make up misleading statistics to prove that America's fiscal burden is being borne by the rich and that the rest of us are freeloaders who don't appreciate that fact. "Half of Americans don't pay taxes" is a perennial meme. But what they leave out is that that statement refers to federal *income* taxes.

---

* The company deducted all of its losses from its GE Capital subsidiary while indefinitely deferring payment on its $10.8 billion in overseas profits.

There are millions of low-income employed people who don't pay income taxes, but they do contribute payroll taxes—among the most regressive form of taxation. According to GOP fiscal theology, however, payroll taxes don't count. Somehow Republicans have convinced themselves that since payroll taxes go into trust funds, like Social Security, they are not real taxes. Likewise, state and local sales taxes do not count, although their effect on a poor person buying necessities such as food is far more regressive than on a millionaire. This explains why Mitt Romney pays federal taxes at an effective rate of 14 percent, while a middle-income earner making sixty-four thousand dollars per year pays 13 percent.

All of these half-truths and outright lies have seeped into popular culture via the corporate-owned business press. Just listen to CNBC for a few hours and you will hear most of them in one form or another. More important politically, Republican myths about taxation have been internalized by millions of economically downscale so-called values voters, who were attracted to the GOP for other reasons (which I will explain later) but now accept this misinformation as sacred dogma. Many people believe their taxes have gone up since the 2008 election, whereas, in reality, thanks to tax provisions in the stimulus bill and Obama's initiative to temporarily reduce federal payroll taxes, they have gone *down*.

When misinformation is not enough to sustain popular support for the GOP's agenda, concealment is needed. One innocuous provision in the Dodd-Frank Wall Street Reform Act of 2010 requires public companies to make a more transparent disclosure of CEO compensation, including bonuses. The bill, which purported to fix the causes of the 2008 financial meltdown (but which had considerable input from industry lobbyists and a Wall Street–friendly Treasury Department), did not even limit the pay of chief officers of public companies but only required full disclosure of that pay. Republicans are determined to repeal this provision. Of course. It would not serve Wall Street's interests if the public took an unhealthy interest in the disparities between their own incomes and those of bank CEOs. As Republican representative Spencer Bachus of Alabama told a home-state newspaper shortly after assuming the chairmanship of the House Financial Services Committee in the wake of the November 2010 election, "In Washington, the view is that the banks are to be regulated, and my view is that Washington and the regulators are there to serve the banks."[8]

On most occasions the GOP prefers to obscure its economic agenda by serving up vague platitudes about their "economic growth agenda" or "creating good jobs and getting the government off Americans' backs." Some Republican candidates are too ignorant of economic policy even to discuss it coherently: Michele Bachmann, while campaigning for the Republican presidential nomination, declared that what the country needed was to return to the tax policies of Ronald Reagan. She was obviously unaware that the tax rates under Reagan were mostly higher than at present.

Herman Cain, once the CEO of Godfather's Pizza, came up with a tax plan that was a masterpiece of marketing, with its simple "9-9-9" label that was vaguely reminiscent of a two-for-one pizza special. Cain would lower all federal income tax rates to a single 9 percent one, set the corporate rate at 9 percent, and levy a national sales tax of 9 percent. It had the sort of meretricious simplicity that would appeal both to the simple-minded and the media. And lo and behold, early on most of the press declared Cain's plan a brilliant campaign move without making any effort to evaluate its likely impact or substantive merits.

Bruce Bartlett, an economist in the Reagan and George H. W. Bush administrations, took the time to crunch the numbers.[9] His conclusion: Cain's plan decreased revenue as it drastically cut the taxes of the wealthy and—here's the kicker—raised taxes on the least well-off. Cain did not actually propose to tax *all* income at 9 percent (so much for his plan's appealing simplicity): He actually lowered the capital gains and dividend tax rates to zero. Generally, the richer the individual is, the more likely his income is derived from capital gains and dividends, which are already taxed at less than half the top marginal income tax rate, than from his salary. This current inequity in the tax code accounts for the fact that the four hundred richest Americans have been paying an average effective federal income tax rate of 17 percent since the passage of the Bush tax cuts—little more than half of what they had paid in the early 1990s—even as their combined income quadrupled. Cain's plan would have sharply increased this disparity.

The usual Republican rationale for reducing tax rates on capital below the rates on labor is that capital gains are "double taxed."* But that is a smokescreen. The American revenue system is about taxing *individual legal entities.* Taxes on an individual, be he a wage earner or sole proprietor of a business, are only levied once; that said, all income the individual gets from whatever source (unless it is specifically exempt) is taxed. Corporations pay taxes only on their profits, a narrower category whose definition is more susceptible to creative bookkeeping. This is how GE can pay zero federal taxes in a given year. Yet that does not preclude its shareholders from realizing capital gains. Those GE shareholders are individual

---

* It is a fine semantic point whether corporations "pay" capital gains. They don't pay them directly insofar as an investor realizes profit by betting correctly on an investment in a company whose market valuation increases before he sells those shares. In a way, that makes the double-taxation argument even more specious, because corporate market valuation is a nontaxable event for the corporation, since it only pays taxes on its profits.

entities who are legally separate from the corporations whose shares they own. That is why they are not liable for corporate mal-feasance or the company's debts. They are taxed once on the income they receive from their investments.

To argue that investors are double taxed is like saying that if Warren Buffett were to give you a billion dollars free and clear, you should pay no taxes on that sum, since Buffett was already taxed on it. Good luck with that argument when you make your not-guilty plea in federal court! The cry of "double taxation" is a perennial red herring designed to let rich speculators skate.

The Tax Policy Center did a distributional analysis of Cain's plan. The center's conclusion:

> A middle-income household making between about $64,000 and $110,000 would get hit with an average tax increase of about $4,300, lowering its after-tax income by more than 6 percent and increasing its average federal tax rate (including income, payroll, estate and its share of the corporate income tax) from 18.8 percent to 23.7 percent. By contrast, a tax-payer in the top 0.1 percent (who makes more than $2.7 million) would enjoy an average tax cut of nearly $1.4 million, increasing his after-tax income by nearly 27 percent. . . . *[A] typical household making more than $2.7 million would pay a smaller share of its income in federal taxes than one making less than $18,000.*[10] [emphasis mine]

This was the brilliant tax plan that briefly spurred Cain's mete-oric rise to Republican front-runner.

At first I wondered: Did Herman Cain dream this plan up himself? If not, who whispered it in his ear, and what interests did that person represent? A little investigating uncovered the fact that

Cain's plan was the brainchild of Rich Lowrie, one of his economic advisers, who lives in Gates Mills, Ohio, a village of twenty-four hundred inhabitants east of Cleveland, and one of the wealthiest suburbs in the country.[11]

Lowrie's day job is as an investment adviser, and he has been involved with such groups as the Koch brothers–funded Club for Growth and Americans for Prosperity. His plan had substantive input from longtime Republican operatives Arthur Laffer (who, with his Laffer Curve, is a forefather of the current generation of crackpot right-wing economists) and Steve Moore, a founder of the Club for Growth and the Free Enterprise Fund, a 501(c)4 organization that promotes the political views of billionaires while remaining tax-exempt.

Still, it is a little surprising that in mid-2011, after the greatest financial meltdown in eighty years, widespread unemployment and destitution, and rising public anger over the greatest income disparity in America since the 1920s, a presidential candidate would tout a plan that would raise taxes on low- and moderate-income earners while drastically reducing them on the wealthy. Republican primary voters are notoriously tolerant of lunatic-fringe proposals, but one would think even they might grow pale at a plan that would raise taxes on the majority of them.

But in reality Cain surged in the polls after unveiling his tax plan. If the media are to be believed, he surged *because* of it. Cain's candidacy, of course, flamed out as a result of unrelated scandals. Still, his tax plan is a stunning illustration of how kamikaze tactics can advance one's political agenda. Several other GOP presidential candidates adopted similar tax proposals. Gingrich's proposal, while less draconian toward the poor and middle class, would sharply lower rates on the wealthy. According to the Tax Policy Center, filers with annual incomes above $1 million would pay tax rates substantially less than those earning $40,000 to $50,000 a year, because in addition to the wealthy having their income tax rates drastically lowered, their investment income is not taxed at all.[12] And federal revenue would fall anywhere from $830 billion to $1.25 trillion per year when fully phased in: This would precipitate an even deeper fiscal crisis, undoubtedly leading to calls for deep cuts in Social Security and Medicare. Perhaps, given his views about those programs, that was partly his intent.

As for Mitt Romney, his initial tax plan had a similar bias: Those making more than $1 million a year would receive an average federal income tax cut of $145,000 by 2015, while those making less than $40,000 would see their federal income taxes increase. At the same time, his scheme would increase deficits by about $180 billion annually by 2015.[13] But apparently that was not enough to satisfy his contributors, so at the end of February 2012 Romney added a 20 percent cut in all income tax rates and a repeal of the alternative minimum tax. The Tax Policy Center estimated that the 20 percent rate cut would add an additional $150 billion to the deficit in 2015 alone. But even Romney looks like a tight-fisted deficit hawk compared to his late-surging rival Rick Santorum, who proposed to sharply lower income taxes and taxes on capital gains and dividends, cut corporate income taxes in half, and eliminate the inheritance tax that falls overwhelmingly on the rich. He would also triple the exemption for dependent children. According to the Committee for a Responsible Federal Budget, Santorum's tax plan would add a staggering $6 trillion to the deficit over the next ten years.[14]

The Republican presidential candidates' fiscal plans shared a common characteristic: They were all riddled with such fantastic assumptions that no neutral observer could come away with any reaction other than that Republicans are so math challenged they could not manage a lemonade stand, let alone the finances of a nation of 310 million people whose government spends $3.5 trillion a year.

While lowering taxes on the wealthy is a well-known formula in the GOP's playbook, Republicans of late have become quite uncharacteristically willing to consider raising taxes. But not on the rich: They are targeting the less well-off.

★

My first contact with a Republican proponent of raising taxes on the poor came in 1999. Two congressional staffers and I were invited over to the Watergate offices of a campaign consultant (I hasten to stress that this was after office hours, on our own time). If elected officials stand on the bottom rung of the public's ladder of esteem, it is probably because the public is not sufficiently familiar with the work of political consultants. This gentleman, Donald Fierce, was representative of the species. His opening formalities consisted of berating us—federal employees who were subject to the Hatch Act and responsible for devoting our office hours solely to the public's business—for the fact that the presidential candidate he was advising, my boss, John Kasich, was falling far behind the George W. Bush campaign juggernaut in the race for the presidential nomination. Then he got down to business.

What policy ideas did we have to relaunch his floundering candidacy? After considerable back and forth, the consultant pitched us one of his own. What with the earned income tax credit and all, the working poor weren't paying any taxes. How about starting a national conversation on the idea that the poor should pay their fair share? I convinced him with some difficulty that a candidate whose entire public career consisted of advocating tax cuts for everybody and tax increases for nobody could hardly be expected to advocate such a policy, nor, I ventured, would it fly with the electorate (this was the electorate of a dozen years ago). But I thought it odd that a savvy GOP fixer would suggest such a policy in the first place.

The first laying of the groundwork in public for the idea of increasing taxes on low-income earners came in a November 2002 *Wall Street Journal* editorial page comment. The working poor, less well-off retirees, and others who do not pay federal income taxes were "lucky duckies," according to the *Journal*. While the paper did not propose any specific remedy for this "problem," it worried that having so many people not paying income taxes would erode popular support for future tax cuts. The *Journal* followed up with two more editorials also using the same infantile phrase to convey its suggestion that a person earning twelve thousand dollars is somehow getting away with something if his earned income tax credit nullifies his income tax liability.

Most Republican officeholders did not come out publicly making the *Journal*'s argument, but sometime later a few, like Jim DeMint and Orin Hatch, occasionally commandeered the Senate chamber to denounce a tax policy that had allegedly allowed almost half of Americans to avoid paying federal income taxes. The whole line of argumentation strikes me as being in bad faith, as it is intended to seduce the listener into confusing people's federal income tax burden with their total tax burden. It leaves out of the equation not only federal payroll taxes, but also those also levied by state and local governments. Less wealthy individuals who are employed, including those who pay no income tax, pay federal payroll taxes that are regressive, while any income above $110,000 is not subject to the Social Security tax. Sales taxes are even more sharply regressive.

Since Obama's election in 2008, Republicans have amped up the "soak the poor" theme. They have been strangely lukewarm about maintaining a payroll tax cut, despite the fact that it would increase the purchasing power of tens of millions of Americans who would have no choice but to recycle the money into the economy in order to buy necessities. That is strange behavior indeed from a party that claims never to have met a tax cut it didn't like; but the Tea Party–infused House Republicans have been in no mood for anything but obstruction. Their pretexts for blocking the extension of the payroll tax cut in December 2011—they wanted a one-year rather than two-month extension, and wanted to offset its cost—are not credible, because they have not insisted that any other tax cuts be offset, and have previously always been more than ready to extend expiring tax cuts for any length of time. Their real intent was to keep making extraneous demands for more concessions until negotiations collapsed. Jeff Flake, a six-term Republican from Arizona, said after the House GOP's back-down that he would "like to see [the deal] unravel completely." He went on to say that "it was a mistake," and that the payroll tax cut should not have been passed in the first place.[15]

In early 2010 the deficit-reduction advisory panel known as the Simpson-Bowles Commission got underway. As a budget committee staffer for one of the commissioners, Senator Judd Gregg of New Hampshire, I assisted the committee on an ad hoc basis. What struck me in the early stages of its deliberations was the apparent bipartisan consensus for a notional tax reform plan that involved, in the words of many of the commission members, "a broadening and flattening of the base." What could that mean? Flattening implied lowering all of the current marginal income tax rates, with the higher rates reduced more than the lower ones. The logical outcome was that wealthier taxpayers would gain more than the less well-off. To offset the loss of revenues, the tax base would have to be broadened: the logic appeared to be that hitherto exempt filers at the lower end of the income scale would have to pay income taxes.

In other words, the commission's notional scheme would largely fulfill the Republicans' tax agenda: lower rates at the top; more people paying at the bottom. But when the commission's staffers set to work to produce a written plan, they had to be conscious of the panel's overriding mandate: to reduce the deficit. So they flattened and broadened the tax base, but to offset the revenue loss they eliminated many deductions from which the wealthy benefit more, and treated capital gains and dividends as ordinary income.

As a result, their draft plan showed a net revenue increase, one which would have gone some distance in reducing future deficits. But even after getting what they said they wanted—lower rates, a broader base, and an elimination of economically inefficient tax deductions and loopholes, along with $4 trillion in outyear deficit reduction—all three House Republican members of the commission voted against the commission recommendations.

This is not the place to discuss the merits and demerits of the Simpson-Bowles deficit-reduction package. Several Democrats voted against it too, showing that the abiding concern of many of them about the deficit is—like the concern of the Republicans—more rhetorical than real. But what is significant is that it was the first serious plan to reveal what Republican priorities are, particularly among House Republicans such as Paul Ryan, whom the press has called a "serious" deficit hawk. Ryan and his two House Republican colleagues rejected a plan embodying the very tax principles—broadening and flattening income tax rates and eliminating loopholes—that they claimed to endorse.*

------

* My boss, Senator Gregg, voted for the Simpson-Bowles recommendations. He was one of the few remaining Republicans in either house of Congress more interested in deficit reduction than in saving the world by banning contraception and making gay marriage illegal. There are even fewer now: He retired at the end of 2010.

During the debt-ceiling negotiations the following summer, the administration offered several deficit-reduction proposals similar to Simpson-Bowles, and House Republicans rejected them all. By this time, with a more right-wing membership following the November 2010 elections, Senate Republicans were also taking a harder line. The result of the debt-ceiling fiasco was that no deficit-reduction deal was made. Congress simply punted the decision to the so-called super committee. When Democrats on that committee offered a plan several months later with the same level of cuts as Simpson-Bowles and only half the revenue increases, Republican committee members from both houses of Congress rejected it out of hand.

One of the reasons for all of these GOP rejections is a habit of political obstructionism that has only grown since early 2009. Most Republicans do not want to give Obama any sort of legislative accomplishment, such as a long-term deficit reduction, even if it would accord with their own political rhetoric. But another reason is that any credible deficit reduction would have to include some revenue increase. Wealthy individuals and big corporations enjoy a greater share of the national income and lower tax rates that at any time since the 1920s. Some Republicans may know that; others, like Michele Bachmann, probably have no more clue about tax policy than quantum physics. But they all know one thing: Their rich contributors must be protected at all costs, and, if possible, the rates on millionaires should be lowered even further.

Smoke and mirrors to the contrary, lowering taxes on the most favored elements of society is the sole object of Republican fiscal policy. They are not serious about deficit reduction. Their behavior has demonstrated it, and their heated rhetoric on the subject is sound and fury signifying nothing. Any serious discussion in this country about deficits and debt must proceed from that fact.

6

WORSHIPPING AT
THE ALTAR OF MARS

**There is no getting around the fact that the GOP
loves war more than it supposedly hates deficits.
But Democrats are furiously playing catch-up.**

★ ★ ★

War is a racket. It always has been. It is possibly the oldest,
easily the most profitable, surely the most vicious. . . . It is the
only one in which the profits are reckoned in dollars
and the losses in lives.

—General Smedley Butler, United States Marine Corps,
twice awarded the Congressional Medal of Honor

While the me-too Democrats have set a horrible example
of late of keeping up with the Joneses when it comes to
waging war, they cannot hope to match the GOP in
their libidinous enthusiasm for invading other countries. John Mc-
Cain went so far as to propose that we mix it up with Russia—a
nuclear-armed state!—during its conflict with Georgia in 2008
(remember "we are all Georgians now," a slogan that did not, fortunately, catch on), and Lindsey Graham has been relentlessly agitat-
ing for attacks on Iran and intervention in Syria. These are not
fringe elements of the party, mind you; they are the leading "defense experts" tapped for the Sunday talk shows. In 2011, about a

month before House Republicans began threatening the credit-worthiness of the United States in their headlong determination to cut trillions of dollars out of the budget, these same Republicans passed a defense appropriations bill that *increased* spending by $17 billion over the prior year's budget.

So much for the GOP's contention that cutting spending and reducing the deficit are their overriding, existential priorities. The Bush administration's principal contribution to sound fiscal policy was to cut taxes while waging a war—something that had never been done before in the country's history—and to leave the cost of the war out of its budget. Republicans have never been very good in math, but the Bush administration set a new low. Since then, regardless of the threat level, regardless of the size of the deficit, the dominant faction in the Republican Party can be counted on every year to seek an increase in the Pentagon's budget.

When the GOP won majorities in the House and Senate in 1994, not long after the collapse of the Warsaw Pact and the dissolution of the Soviet Union, the U.S. armed forces had recently demonstrated their crushing military superiority in the Gulf War. One would have thought this might suffice to convince any remaining skeptics that we had all the military hardware we needed. The deficit was growing seemingly intractably, and the GOP had won the 1994 election on a sweeping platform of spending cuts and the promise of a balanced budget. This was the bedrock of Newt Gingrich's "Contract with America." To balance the budget without raising taxes would have required significant cuts in almost every budgetary category. The Department of Defense (DOD) budget—which accounts for half of all discretionary spending—would have to be cut, or at least held flat. I knew the numbers because my boss was the incoming House Budget Committee chairman, John Kasich, who was charged with producing a balanced budget. Yet as soon as the new Republican Congress was seated, the House and Senate Armed Services committees demanded that the Pentagon's six-year spending plan be increased by at least $120 billion.

I vividly recall how in January 1995 the committee chairmen hashed out their differences in the Speaker's office. Kasich told Newt and his counterparts on the Armed Services Committee that defense spending would have to be placed "under the same microscope" as all other spending if the budget was ever to be balanced. The newly minted House Armed Services Committee chairman, Floyd Spence, responded with an emotional tirade that ended with his saying that Kasich—who had spent twelve years on the Armed Services Committee—was "destroying the defense of this country." In the end, Floyd didn't get the whole loaf: He did get a modest increase of $6 billion that year, when every other department was being cut. For several years thereafter, Republicans increased every budget the Pentagon submitted by a few billion dollars, enough to poke a finger in the eye of the Clinton administration but not enough to risk a presidential veto. I occasionally found myself wondering how our political system could allow people like Floyd Spence, a man of exquisitely unsound judgment, to get into a position of significant influence on U.S. national security policy.

A cynic might conclude that this militaristic enthusiasm could be explained by the simple fact that Pentagon contractors spread a lot of bribe money around Capitol Hill. That is of course true, but there is more to it than that. Some members of Congress will claim that they are protecting constituents' jobs, but even that doesn't really explain it. The wildly uneven concentration of defense contracts and military bases means that some areas, such as Washington, D.C., and San Diego, are heavily dependent on DOD spending, but in most of the country the balance is a net negative: More is paid out in taxes to support the Pentagon than comes back in local contracts.

Economic justifications for Pentagon spending are even less persuasive when one considers that the $600 billion spent every year on the DOD generates comparatively few jobs per dollar spent. The days of Rosie the Riveter are long gone; most weapons projects now require very little touch labor. Instead, a disproportionate share is siphoned off into high-cost R&D (from which the civilian economy benefits little), exorbitant management expenditures, whopping overhead, and out-and-out padding—including, of course, the money that flows back into the coffers of political campaigns. A dollar appropriated for highway construction, health care, or education will create many more jobs than a dollar appropriated for Pentagon weapons procurement: The jobs argument is thoroughly specious.*

Take away the cash nexus and there remains a strong psychological predisposition toward war and militarism in a large part of the GOP. This tic, greatly exacerbated in the immediate aftermath of September 11 and alarmingly persistent since then, undoubtedly arises from a neurotic need to demonstrate toughness. It dovetails perfectly with the belligerent tough-guy affect one constantly hears on right-wing talk radio. Militarism springs from a psychological deficit that requires an endless series of enemies both foreign and domestic. So it is not surprising that the party that gave us Joe McCarthy and red-baiting should embrace the war on terror. To borrow the author Chris Hedges's formulation, war is a force that gives them meaning.

The results of the last decade of unbridled militarism, and of

---

* A University of Massachusetts study claims that several alternative ways of spending money would produce anywhere from 35 percent to 138 percent more jobs than spending the same amount on DOD. (http://www.peri .umass.edu/fileadmin/pdf/published_study/PERI_military_spend ing_2011.pdf).

the Democrats' cowardly or opportunistic refusal to oppose it, have been disastrous, both strategically and fiscally. It has damaged our respect for the Bill of Rights and severely impaired our standing in the world. Unfortunately, because of the toxic political dynamic prevailing in Washington, the militarism and the promiscuous intervention it has given rise to seem likely to abate only when the Treasury is exhausted and creditors balk at renewing loans, as happened to hubristic military empires in the past, such as Great Britain in the period between World War II and the Suez crisis or the Spanish Empire in its long slide from world power in the eighteenth century. *or the Dutch Revolution*

By a process of self-selection, acculturation, and groupthink, a majority of the members of Congress currently sitting on the defense committees of both the House and Senate have become rigid advocates of ever higher military spending, even when this position conflicts with their much advertised insistence on the need to rein in the national debt and their tiresome and hypocritical rhetorical claims that we must not leave fiscal burdens on the backs of our children. Many of these people would be similarly disposed even if there were no juicy DOD contracts producing jobs in their districts or states or helping to finance their next campaigns. The staffs of these committees have been conditioned by a similar process and often think like their bosses; many are military retirees with an emotional connection to their old services. So how did I, who worked most of my career on military issues, come to have such skeptical opinions about the defense establishment of this country?

When I arrived on the Hill during Reagan's first term, I was a conventional, mainstream Republican. I believed in the notion of peace through strength. At that time the slogan translated quite literally into spending more money on the Pentagon. The Soviet Union had invaded Afghanistan not long before, and the Warsaw

Pact seemed like a powerful and monolithic threat. I did not know then (and was probably too naïvely trusting to have believed it even if someone had tried to dispel my illusions) that the intelligence agencies were systematically inflating the Soviet threat, and that the Soviet military was far weaker than we imagined.

The senior appointees at the CIA—chief among them Robert Gates, who was then deputy director for intelligence—became so enamored of the concept of the Soviet threat that they somehow missed the fact that the collapse of the Warsaw Pact lay only a few years ahead.* The Pentagon's Defense Intelligence Agency was equally enthusiastic about inflating threats. Every year during the 1980s the Pentagon produced a lavishly illustrated publication, printed on coated paper, called *Soviet Military Power*. Many of the illustrations were color sketches of the fearsome hardware the Soviets supposedly had, or would have in the future (as with defense contractor brochures, the goal was to make the reader feel that the visual representation was real and not someone's fanciful projection). According to the cosmology of *Soviet Military Power*, the Soviets were not ten feet tall; they were twenty feet tall, with death rays projecting from their eyes.

The first crack in my credulity came in 1985, upon hearing an unclassified symposium on the Soviet Union that was held in Annapolis, Maryland. One of the experts was Murray Feshbach, then a demographer for the U.S. Census Bureau. Rather than interpreting the state of Soviet power from satellite photographs of missile fields or shipyards, he looked at available data about life expectancy at birth, fertility rates, infant mortality, nutrition, and so on, and

---

* Senators attending the hearings for Gates's confirmation as CIA director in 1991 brushed aside testimony from former CIA employees about his intelligence distortions because the fix was in, and President George H. W. Bush was not to be denied his nominee.

came to the conclusion that the USSR was a walking corpse—that it could not sustain itself as a superpower for much longer. I don't know whether he influenced any of the other congressional staffers in attendance, but it made me begin to question the prevailing wisdom critically.

My doubts as to the proper management of our military-industrial complex here at home began to grow around the same time. I worked in a congressional office representing a district in Ohio where the B-1 bomber—a project the Carter administration had canceled and the Reagan administration had revived as a cornerstone of its buildup policy—was a significant source of employment. One can generally tell which weapon system is built in a congressman's district by the contractor models on the office desks, the pictures on the walls, and the frequent presence of lobbyists from the company that builds the system. In our case, it was all B-1 all the time.

By the late 1980s, as the first production examples began to enter service, a funny thing happened—although it would not have been funny to the taxpayer who was funding the plane at a then considerable cost of $280 million each. The aircraft's defensive avionics, which were supposed to detect and neutralize enemy electronic systems seeking to find and destroy the B-1, were seriously interfering with the plane's own offensive avionics, whose goal was to help it find enemy targets and attack them. In other words, the contractors had managed to build a self-jamming bomber.

Three planes were written off in crashes shortly after the B-1 entered operational status. Two of these were caused by a poor design in the fuel or hydraulic lines. It soon became evident that needless secrecy surrounded the crash reports: The services hid the details even from Armed Services Committee members with the requisite clearances and an obvious need to know what had happened. The B-1 was AWOL in the first Gulf war, and when it took part in operations in Kosovo in 1999, it flew only after older aircraft—like the antique B-52 it had been intended to replace—had already suppressed Serbian air defenses. There are dozens of weapons systems like the B-1 rattling around in the Pentagon's closet—cold war dinosaurs that are overpriced, underperforming, and unreliable. Every one of them has a coalition of congressional supporters who protect it from conception until decades later, when the military retires it from service; and even then, many in Congress will lobby for a reversal. Keeping these dinosaurs operating assures jobs for constituents. But at what cost to the rest of us?

What of the ethics of all this? One could take a charitable view that all the actors in a tragicomedy like the B-1 were fallible human beings who believed in the magnitude of the foreign threat and were merely optimistic about their ability to manage an important national project. The services, for their part, foster a can-do mentality among their members that does not invite naysayers. Some incidents, however, leave no doubt about an absence of good faith and honesty, because they verge upon the criminal. The official investigation into the explosion of the number-two gun turret of the USS *Iowa* on April 19, 1989, which killed forty-seven sailors, was one such incident.

The Navy's briefing on the preliminary investigation to the professional staff of the House Armed Services Committee and to the staffers of the members of the committee was a *Through the Looking Glass* event. The admiral in charge of the investigation, accompanied by the phalanx of uniformed coat holders and chart flippers who always escort the Pentagon's top brass, claimed to have it all figured out.

The explosion was an intentional act of sabotage by a Navy enlisted man killed in the explosion who had become suicidal when his homosexual relationship with another crew member had gone bad. The perpetrator had fashioned a detonator and placed it in the firing chamber of the gun barrel. The case was all wrapped up. No defects in equipment, training, or doctrine. Up went my hand. "Uh, if the guy was suicidal, why didn't he kill himself by the usual practice of jumping off the ship's fantail at night? What's the evidence for an elaborate plan to take out his shipmates?"

The admiral had an answer for that. The FBI had assisted the Navy in carrying out the investigation and had put together a psychological profile that was, we were told, both empirical and scientific. Hartwig (Clayton Hartwig was the alleged perpetrator) was a man who would do such a thing. It just fits his profile; believe us, it's true. Other questions followed from equally skeptical staffers. There was something a little unsettling about the admiral's insistence that the tragedy was a criminal act by a man who was conveniently dead. To this day there is no definitive proof as to the cause of the *Iowa* disaster. But tests by Sandia National Laboratories and a review of the evidence by the Government Accountability Office strongly suggest the cause to have been either improper Navy training in loading the guns or defective powder. For the Navy to admit this, however, was intolerable; far better to blame a dead man.

The *Iowa* incident was a perfect counterpoint to my one previous professional experience with the Navy. For nine months in 1988 I attended courses at the Naval War College's Washington, D.C., campus. It was one of the most intellectually fulfilling experiences of my life. The students—mainly lieutenants, lieutenant commanders, and commanders, or their Marine Corps rank equivalents, were without exception bright, inquisitive, and skeptical. But something happens when officers rise into the flag ranks, and the same process occurs in the other services as well.

As the cold war drew to a close the defense establishment had evolved into a rigid, bureaucratic institution strangely emulating the defunct Soviet system it believed it had vanquished. Its real mission had become inwardly focused: to preserve the status, privileges, and prerogatives it had enjoyed. The Pentagon developed a whole vocabulary to enable this. There is no such thing in the military as a problem; there are only "issues" or "challenges." Mistakes or errors never occur. I recall watching one prototype missile test launch that blew up perhaps three seconds after liftoff. A general pronounced it "a nominal success." As the Pentagon status quo grew more entrenched, the rest of government, unfortunately, began to emulate its behavior.

This dysfunctional mutation bore evil fruit in the first decade of the twenty-first century: the Pat Tillman cover-up; Abu Ghraib; concealed atrocities; bad conditions for wounded soldiers at the Walter Reed army hospital; harassment of service personnel with post-traumatic stress disorder (PTSD). These and other cases tend to follow a set script: The incident is followed by the inevitable cover-up and denial; as the cover-up unravels, some small-fry might be thrown to the wolves; then comes absolution by means of an internally generated, phony "reform."

This procedure is now standard both in military departments and civilian agencies. If there is a procurement scandal, the solution is the Band-Aid of toothless "acquisition reform," leaving the same people to administer the programs. The failures of high-level policy judgments that played the biggest part in allowing 9/11 to occur were disguised as the much less significant failures of intelligence collection, analysis, and interagency sharing. Why? If the public were to blame policy judgments at the top, George W. Bush, Dick Cheney, Condoleezza Rice, and several cabinet secretaries might be on the hook. But if the fault could be placed on operatives lower down the food chain, as well as on "institutional failures" of the bureaucracy, Congress and the public could be distracted by the monkey motion of "reform" and government reorganization. This is how we ended up with even more bureaucracy in the form of the Office of the Director of National Intelligence, not to mention the monstrosity of the Department of Homeland Security.

The dysfunctions of our uniformed military, our intelligence agencies (85 percent of whose funding flows through military budgets), and the rest of government did not arise overnight, and they did not form in a vacuum. They are partially the products of an odd and seldom-remarked schizophrenia that has grown up in our political culture. There are many people active in politics who claim they would man the barricades to fight to the death against socialism. But these are almost always the same people who also say they adore the U.S. military, which is probably the largest—certainly the most lavishly funded—socialist institution remaining on Earth since the collapse of the USSR and the transformation of China.

America's military bases are separate little worlds with their own law enforcement and traffic rules—not to mention their own grocery stores (commissaries), big-box stores (PXs), and so on, down to their own DOD Dependents School system, child care centers, housing, and comprehensive health care system—all of them run by the government. There are important historical reasons why these facilities arose, having to do with the low salaries of the old draft military and the frequent remoteness of military bases from retail business, schools, and essential services (on the frontier or overseas, for example). These facilities remain an important factor in the retention of military personnel, particularly those with dependents, to this day. But it is a socialist, or at least highly welfarist state, arrangement.* Today, with the advent of the all-volunteer force, salaries are much higher; according to the Congressional Budget Office, military pay averages around the seventy-fifth percentile when compared to civilian jobs with comparable skills. Other studies by the CBO have demonstrated that in several cases, such as the commissaries (the huge retail grocery chains operated by the DOD), a cash allowance would give service members the same level of grocery benefit that they enjoy now—at substantially less cost. Yet whenever the Pentagon offers a proposal to change these arrangements—such as letting annual health care premiums for retirees rise with inflation (they have remained the same since 1995)—Congress invariably rejects it, with the free-market, fiscal hawk Republicans usually leading the opposition.

This same sort of military socialism prevails in regions of the country heavily dependent on military contracts. Loudoun County, Virginia, an outer suburb of Washington, D.C., offers a perfect example of this ethos. It is the richest county in the United States when measured by median household income.† It is very enthusiastically Republican.[1] And the number-one and number-two military contractors in the country, Lockheed Martin and Northrop Grumman, are located there. Fairfax County, the county next to Loudoun, has the second-highest median household income in the

---

* During the debate over the health care bill in 2009, a former colleague who had gone to work in the defense industry mentioned a co-worker of his— retired military—who had criticized "socialist Obamacare." As a military retiree this person would have paid an annual premium of $230 for his health insurance if he were single or $460 for himself and his family. Yes, they were earned benefits, but taxpayer subsidized nevertheless.

† Some lists count the independent city of Falls Church, Virginia, also in the Washington suburbs, as a county. If so, it would outrank Loudoun in per capita income. It, too, is heavily dependent on military spending.

country. The fifth-ranked military contractor, General Dynamics, is based there.

It is no anomaly that areas of the country heavily involved in military contracting are so wealthy. A study by the Project On Government Oversight found that in thirty-three of thirty-five job categories the government paid billions more to private companies than they would have paid government employees to do the same job.[2] On average they paid about twice as much. A source in industry has told me that DynCorp employees acting as security guards at military bases are obtained under contracts paying the company *four* dollars for every dollar the guard gets paid. Beyond the extravagant profit margins involved, this arrangement reveals that the military can no longer guard its own facilities with its own personnel.* Since the 1990s, our army can no longer even feed itself whenever it takes the field; service contractors such as Halliburton do that for the usual exorbitant markup. And the taxpayer takes a further hit, because the contractors often hire retired military personnel (or lure serving personnel to retire by offering them more pay); this means that these ostensibly private employees are frequently getting paid both a salary from the government that is washed through the contracting company, which takes its cut, *and* a government pension. To top off the bargain, this process is how the military loses some of its most experienced personnel.

The huge, uncompetitive profit margins that military contracting generates explain why the richest areas of the country are the most dependent on government. Yet the peculiar sociology of the

---

* The military would claim that they cannot have soldiers pull guard duty because they don't have enough service members to fight wars and perform domestic functions. The rebuttal is that they cannot afford to recruit more soldiers because they are locked into expensive service contracts (and useless weapons systems) that crowd out the rest of their budget.

military-industrial complex allows for a dependent population that disproportionately thinks of itself as small-government conservative. This is particularly true in outer-suburban counties like Loudoun that are rural enough to maintain the illusion of a free Jeffersonian yeomanry among the many contractor personnel whose McMansions have been sprouting up in what was once Virginia's horse country.

Republicans, in their statements on military policy, have taken to making a ritual genuflection to the notion that our elected leaders should follow the advice of military commanders—unless, of course, those commanders give advice that conflicts with what Republicans want. When in 2008 President Bush announced the scheduling of a final troop withdrawal from Iraq for the end of 2011, many Republicans breathed a sigh of relief that the albatross of an unpopular war soon would be removed from their necks. But when on October 21, 2011, Obama announced the definitive date as being December 31, 2011,* GOP presidential candidates issued harsh statements condemning the president for ceding ground to the enemy and saying that United States forces should remain in Iraq as long as the generals say we should stay.

The GOP seems to have forgotten—even more so than the Democrats, who periodically become enamored of a Wesley Clark or an Eric Shinseki—that our constitutional system of government absolutely and unconditionally requires civilian control of the military. That George Washington faced down his mutinous officers at Newburgh, New York, stands as one of the lesser-known milestones in the development of American self-government. If only it were

---

* Never mind for the moment Obama's own hypocrisy in taking political credit for the withdrawal when his own administration had been negotiating with Iraq's government for the right to keep troops there after 2011.

studied more frequently. Washington's rationale was that the army should not be allowed to overthrow or overawe the republic's properly established magistrates, else a militarized despotism would reign. This was the position of our first president, revered now in ritual as the father of his country but little remembered for his supreme accomplishment: saving the very idea of a self-governing republic.

Had Civil War policy been left in the hands of a George McClellan or an Ambrose Burnside, rather than the duly elected president, Abraham Lincoln, a disaster would have resulted that would most likely have left the country cleaved in two. Franklin Roosevelt's mostly political decision to invade North Africa in November 1942 turned out to be a good call. Harry Truman wisely fired General Douglas MacArthur and prevented a bloody and nasty Korean War from becoming a world conflagration. President Kennedy's rejection of his generals' near unanimous advice to invade Cuba may have prevented a nuclear war with the Soviet Union. But for all of Lyndon Johnson's domestic accomplishments, a second term was foreclosed to him because he listened to General William Westmoreland's fantasies of an imminently achievable victory in Vietnam. How have we forgotten all of this?

I met many generals in my career. The great majority of them thoroughly knew their jobs, were well informed, and had a broad perspective on the landscape of national security. But one thing they did not have: a certificate of election by the American people. Whatever the compelling military reasons for their advocacy of an operation, they might not fully understand the overriding diplomatic reasons a particular plan should not be pursued or the domestic fiscal complications that might make it on balance a no go. As professional executors of a given mission, they focus on that mission, and naturally, they want to complete it with 100 percent success, as they define that. But a president must juggle a vast array of competing priorities, not least the ultimate priority of our present fiscal predicament: No mission can be sound if fulfilling it assumes resources the Treasury does not have.

As a former hired hand of government I was acutely conscious that I, too, did not hold a certificate of election. Whatever brilliant idea I might come up with, it had to be vetted by somebody who had to stand before voters. I am reasonably sure that the vast majority of our military officers understand that precept. Their commissions to lead troops in battle come from the people through their elected leaders, and their promotions must be confirmed by the Senate.

It is according to this principle that public officeholders should not sanctify the military judgment of commanders as the only criterion by which a national security policy may be formulated. Vigorous, assertive, and intelligent civilian control of the military is more important now than ever before. The United States no longer has a draft military that would be more sensitive to public sentiment, particularly in a time of war. Since September 11, 2001, the nation has been more or less continuously at war, with a volunteer military from which the general public is increasingly remote. Since 2000 the military budget has almost doubled, even after excluding the amounts spent on the wars themselves. Budgets have risen effortlessly not merely because Congress does not exercise proper oversight, but because it exacerbates the situation by throwing money at every real, claimed, or imaginary military deficiency. Even some members of Congress who are privately skeptical of the military's claims, and opposed to the announced war policy, have voted for defense spending bills, because they think that to do otherwise is politically dangerous.

This unquestioning adoration of the military, and of the military brass in particular, can reach comic lengths. Kasich, a rare skeptic of military claims, once said in frustration about a colleague who was chairman of a subcommittee of the House Armed Services Committee: "You know, if a general came into his office and said the sky is green and the grass is blue, old ＿＿ would look out the window and say, 'General, I believe you're right!'"

What is not so funny are the real-world consequences of this adulation. Every time General David Petraeus appeared before a congressional committee, whether to testify about Iraq or Afghanistan or to be confirmed as CIA director, the hearings were largely a waste of time. Members of Congress burned through large segments of their time-limited question periods by tossing verbal kisses to the witness and going on about what a patriot Petraeus was. There was little time to ask serious questions about the strategy of our trillion-dollar military engagement in the Muslim world and to explore alternatives. The fawning of military cheerleaders such as Joe Lieberman and Lindsey Graham reached such extravagant lengths as would have made Caesar blush. I am not advocating rudeness to generals or the kind of witness badgering one recalls from Senator Joe McCarthy's days. But if the public wants the military to perform better, give more prudent advice to its civilian leadership, and spend taxpayer money more wisely, it must elect a Congress that will dial down a few notches its habitual and childish "we support the troops!" mantra and start asking skeptical questions—and not accepting bland evasions or appeals to patriotism as a response.

Congress's worshipful attitude toward the military has come at a particularly inauspicious time and exacerbates harmful trends within the uniformed services. As military budgets have risen, the cancer of careerism, always present, has metastasized in the officer corps. Obviously, professional officers should be well compensated. But a general does not retire poor: The base annual salary of a major general is $163,428, and that does not include thousands of dollars in additional spending power due to tax-free housing and subsistence allowances, subsidized grocery shopping, and free medical care. A retiring general can count on "retired pay" (as service members call their pensions) worth about two thirds of his base pay.

And unlike Douglas MacArthur, these old soldiers do not fade away. According to Bloomberg News, "The top 10 U.S. defense contractors have 30 retired senior officers or former national security officials serving on their boards. Press releases issued by those companies since 2008 announced the hiring of almost two dozen prominent flag officers or senior officials as high-ranking executives." The article also states that senior executives at the largest U.S. defense contractors are paid from $1 million to $11 million a year.*

The revolving-door nature of the military-industrial complex guarantees cost overruns, schedule slips, and poor weapon performance. Suppose an officer is a year from retirement: Is he going to blow the whistle on shoddy performance by a contractor? Both he and the contractor are conscious that a seven-figure paycheck might lie in his future (salvaging a contract potentially worth billions of dollars certainly merits the investment of a few million). Every precept in the military's code of conduct demands that he blow the whistle, but a secure, even lavish future can sorely tempt one's less noble instincts. In addition, the chances that a contractor will actually be prosecuted are vanishingly small. Federal conflict-

---

* Enlisted personnel separating from the service typically face a far different career future: Iraq and Afghanistan veterans have endured a substantially higher unemployment rate than the national average.

of-interest laws exist but are filled with loopholes. No word has to be spoken by either party. Neither the contractor nor the officer has to commit an overt act; the deed is accomplished instead by doing nothing.

Occasionally, someone gets caught. In 2004, a federal court sentenced Darleen Druyun, a senior Air Force procurement official, to nine months in prison for favoring Boeing in contract negotiations for a $20 billion aircraft tanker leasing deal (a procurement scandal in itself) at the same time she was speaking to Boeing about a postgovernment job. But that was the tip of the iceberg. The Commission on Wartime Contracting, created by Congress in 2008, undertook three years of investigations into contracting practices in Iraq and Afghanistan (tasks that the House and Senate Armed Services committees, as permanent committees of Congress, should have undertaken themselves). In August 2011 the commission issued a report concluding that waste, fraud, and abuse in wartime contracting resulted in losses of $31 billion to $60 billion. The estimating range is so broad because the Department of Defense, with a laughably inept system of financial management, has a hard time even detecting overpayments.

The crowning irony is that Congress often has epic fights on the floors of the two chambers over some $10 million program in a domestic agency. One could more easily accept the principle that every little bit helps, and that even a program funded at a few million annually should be rigorously scrubbed, if our national legislature did not let $600 billion defense bills pass with so little genuine scrutiny, and allow tens of billions of dollars in aggregate waste flow to contractors. Congress operates like a university faculty: The smaller the stakes, the more heated the argument.

I saw this many times in practice over the years. Congress dutifully funded, with little floor debate, the Future Combat Systems—

a family of Army combat vehicles—a program the Army estimated would cost $160 billion (independent estimates were as high as $230 billion). The funding continued year after year, until in 2009 the Pentagon finally pulled the plug on the flawed and gold-plated program. But when the issue involves a $2 million line item for a bike path or highway beautification, a vigorous floor debate ensues. The point is not to defend bike paths or highway beautification; with an annual budget deficit in excess of $1 trillion, it is hard to defend them. But if we cannot afford them, how can Congress continue to fund the F-35 Joint Strike Fighter, whose total program cost has risen to $382 billion, despite repeated Government Accountability Office warnings that it was rushed into production despite serious development flaws?

★

The Constitution provides for separate and independent branches of government: the separation of powers. The executive branch zealously upholds the concept of independent presidential power; its battery of lawyers doggedly fights off any perceived encroachment on its turf. The Bush administration set the gold standard for this sort of behavior, although the Obama presidency is now giving it a run for its money, particularly in the realm of war powers. The judicial branch—mostly—follows a similar policy of jealously guarding its prerogatives. Congress, however, has heaved out the window its constitutional responsibilities both to declare war and to raise and support armies, as well as to demand that the Pentagon adhere to the appropriations and accountability clauses of the Constitution.

This abdication is partly the result of emotionally immature legislators getting swept away with enthusiasm for military adventure, much as European parliaments did in the summer of 1914. It is partly an avoidance of responsibility. But it is also, at least to some degree, due to obscure institutional arrangements that the general public has hardly heard of. The most visible and extensive executive branch liaison offices on Capitol Hill are those of the uniformed services. They provide a permanent and continual presence in the halls of Congress to lobby for their priorities. Even more submerged is the fact that many if not all members of Congress assigned to the defense committees have a "military fellow": an active-duty military officer serving a tour of duty in a Capitol Hill office. If they all wore their uniforms rather than Brooks Brothers, they would make Capitol Hill look like Fort Bragg.

So what's wrong with that? We are all part of the same government, aren't we? To be sure, the vast majority are honest people performing their assignment. A couple of them I knew more than casually, and they were good guys. But the fact that they are serving in one branch of government while being paid by an agency from another branch, and especially one with enormous institutional power and a relentless agenda, inevitably creates a conflict of interest. The sheer institutional pervasiveness of the military in the legislative branch is itself a reason for caution. There is nothing sinister about the fact that the agenda of one branch of government will conflict with the prerogatives of another branch; James Madison foresaw that possibility over two centuries ago. But it is problematic to place young military officers in an assignment that requires dual loyalty.

The matter does not end there. The congressional defense committees are loaded with people who retired from the military and are now congressional employees. Well, what of it? Isn't that where the expertise is? Most civilians don't consider how much an entire career spent in the military inspires a strong loyalty to one's service. Congress should do a better job of nurturing its own talent, as well as better utilizing its support agencies, such as the Congressional Research Service and the Congressional Budget Office, along with the Government Accountability Office.

★

One of the most noisome phenomena in the Washington culture pertaining to military matters is the chicken hawk. The great majority of those serving in the military are motivated by patriotism and see the profession of arms as a job to do as well as they can. Their patriotism is usually mixed with judgments we all would feel if exposed at any length to Pentagon bureaucracy: that it is—like all bureaucracies—at its most benign like *Sergeant Bilko* and at its worst like *Catch-22*. Anyone who has had a beer at the enlisted club of a military base will know that most of the troops are not starry-eyed idealists about their trade. Having the skepticism of the realist does not keep them from doing their duty, but it does check the mindless boosterism of those who choose to avoid military service while loudly advocating war. There is nothing like the prospect of getting killed or maimed to concentrate the mind.

The chicken hawk phenomenon probably exists in other cultures and can be found throughout American history; Mark Twain addressed the same pathology over a hundred years ago when he wrote the passage about "the Loud Little Handful" in *The Mysterious Stranger,* about those who agitate for war. But the business of chicken-hawk advocacy has become a well-paid and influential vocation in modern America. Its principal venues are the neoconservative *Weekly Standard*, the supposedly liberal *New Republic*, the editorial page of the *Wall Street Journal*, and increasingly that of the *Washington Post*. It is also entrenched in think tanks such as the American Enterprise Institute and the Heritage Foundation. If you ever wondered how the United States came to be embroiled simultaneously in two major wars and a half dozen covert ones in the past decade, the cheerleading of Washington's laptop commandos, with their disproportionate influence in major media, has been a major factor. This is not to say that only those with military experience should have standing to discuss military policy. That would contravene the principle of civilian control of the military. But when a self-appointed group of experts almost entirely innocent of military service relentlessly advocates getting this country into one war after another, it is time to be on guard and hold on to our wallets. Besides which, their judgments are almost always wrong.

Over the last five years we have spent more money on the military—in real, inflation-adjusted dollars—than during any other five-year period since World War II. That includes the late 1960s, when the United States simultaneously faced a peer competitor with ten thousand nuclear weapons *and* sent half a million troops to Vietnam. The Pentagon is spending recklessly at a time of fiscal crisis when America's debt has been downgraded. Despite what secretaries Gates and Panetta have claimed, the DOD budget has been, next to the Bush tax cuts, the single greatest contributor to the drastic swing from surplus to deficit since 2001. When debt-service costs are included, the wars have cost about $1.7 trillion. Additionally, the Pentagon has spent about $1 trillion above inflation on its nonwar budget. Adding debt service makes that about $1.3 trillion, for a grand total of roughly $3 trillion added to the debt, courtesy of DOD. (For a quick comparison, the total Pentagon budget in the last year of the Clinton administration was $287 billion. In the last year of the Bush administration it had reached $665 billion, including the cost of the wars.)

Yet ever since the rejection of the Simpson-Bowles deficit-reduction package in December 2010, as we have been struggling to get the budget under control, every interest group inside the

Washington Beltway has been forecasting imminent doom if one cent is cut from Pentagon budgets.[3] Why? The service chiefs' doom-saying testimony to Congress has been standard for at least the three decades that I was on the Hill: Deliberate threat inflation, based in part on serious intelligence failures, has been the genesis of wasted billions. China-as-military-threat is again in vogue at the Pentagon and in Congress, though the Iranian bogeyman currently has the upper hand. There is a threat from China, but it comes not from the rust-bucket aircraft carrier it bought from Russia. China now owns about $1 trillion in U.S. Treasury securities—36 percent of all foreign holdings. According to the International Monetary Fund (IMF), China is poised to pass the United States in gross domestic product by 2016. That is the real threat we face, not death rays and stealth air fleets. If you want to gaze upon the threat China poses, not because of any inherent evil on its part but because of our own tax policy, spending priorities, "free-trade" ideology, and the general indifference of our elites, go to Youngstown, or Toledo, or some other postindustrial wasteland.[4, 5]

The United States spends about as much on its military as all other countries in the world combined. It could shave a trillion off a projected $6.1 trillion in spending over the next decade and still be miles ahead of the next power, or of any conceivable combination of powers. But what about another 9/11, ask the Cassandras? In 2001, the United States already spent as much on its military as everyone else in the world, but that did not help prevent 9/11. That disaster was an intelligence failure: That is, a failure of our intelligence agencies to some degree, but far more a failure of the cognitive intelligence and good judgment of our elected so-called leaders.

The United States is now a bloated military empire on the cusp of steady and irrevocable economic decline. Historically, the danger in such cases is that when the fiscal stability of the empire begins to weaken, the governing elites double down on the very policies of military profligacy that caused the fiscal crisis in the first place. And that appears to be what the people who run America would like to do.

This doubling down on failure should come as no surprise: Powerful entrenched interests will never be tamed without a bitter and protracted struggle. The trigger for the latest round of scare tactics has been the automatic defense cuts that are supposed to ensue in 2013 if the congressional super committee could not find alternative deficit-reduction measures (it couldn't). As soon as the reality that the Pentagon might have to take budget cuts began to seep into the bureaucracy's consciousness, the drumbeat began. Secretary of Defense Leon Panetta, a supposed liberal and alleged fiscal hawk, made a preposterous statement comparing himself in his efforts to prevent defense reductions to General Anthony McAuliffe at the Battle of the Bulge saying "nuts" to the enemy. We are supposed to infer that anyone wanting to cut Pentagon extravagance for the sake of the national debt is akin to the *Wehrmacht* attacking American patriots who are holding beleaguered Bastogne.

Iran's alleged nuclear capability quickly became a feature of the increased threat mongering. For most of my three decades on Capitol Hill, threat inflators have claimed that Iran has been two years away from possessing nuclear weapons. Recycled rumors, half-truths, disinformation from foreign intelligence agencies like that of Saudi Arabia and Israel, and exaggerations have been a consistent feature of these scare tactics. By the end of 2011 these allegations were taking on an increasingly hysterical tone. The *Washington Post*, ever a bellwether of the establishment, printed an editorial demanding a sanctions regime against Iran so strict it would amount to a blockade equivalent to war, because the only other alternative was a military attack "forced on the United States."[6]

One thing that could further ratchet up the hype would be to let people who are either woefully misinformed about the world or shallow opportunists, or both, ventilate their opinions about Iran and treat their ruminations as national news. The interminable series of Republican presidential candidate debates was one more venue to make us very, very scared of Iran, and the candidates obliged. Asking a Republican candidate about Iran is almost as good as giving him a large campaign donation: It gives him a chance to show "toughness" and "seriousness" (meaning reckless belligerence) on foreign policy issues; appeal to the Israel lobby for votes and money (it is a quadrennial spectacle to watch the candidates outbid each other to the point of getting to the right even of Israel's Likud government); and devise crackbrained schemes to deal with the potentially ruinous economic consequences of an oil blockade of Iran. (Gingrich believed we could snap our fingers and quickly replace the 2.4 million barrels of oil per day that Iran exports.)

But the larger objective, beyond specific policies, is to blanket the American public with a message of fear. As long as we are fearful, as long as there is an endless list of threats, Pentagon spending can never be cut, PATRIOT Act provisions can never be repealed, and the United States will forever have the right and duty to meddle in every corner of the world. By coincidence (or not), the same day the *Post* clamored for action against Iran it ran a story that exemplifies the propaganda techniques of the national security complex.[7] The story explained that al Qaeda targets had dwindled as its leaders had been killed or captured: "We have rendered the organization that brought us 9/11 operationally ineffective," said an anonymous senior U.S. counterterrorism official. So we're on the verge of victory, right? No: "[T]he terrorist group will remain a major security threat for years." And now it looks as if the scene will shift to Yemen: The terrorist group there is a "significantly greater threat." Moreover, we have to be concerned about lone-wolf attacks inside the United States as well. The Orwellian nature of these contradictory messages is plain: Our leaders' objective is to convince us that the sacrifice of blood and treasure has been worth it by depicting victory as within reach; nevertheless, the threat will endlessly mutate and require enormous budgets and nonstop war for the indefinite future.

Final victory is a mirage our leaders say we must chase as it recedes to the horizon. History is littered with powers that followed this ruinous path: the Spanish Empire, the Dutch Republic, the British Empire, the Soviet Union. Vaunting rhetoric to the contrary, our military policies of the last decade have left us less prosperous, less secure, and less free. A course correction is desperately needed, regardless of what our entrenched, out-of-touch, and corrupt Beltway elites think is good for us.

7

MEDIA COMPLICITY

Despite the widely believed myth of its liberalism,
over the last thirty years the media landscape has
become increasingly wired to favor Republicans. The
press's current combination of fake objectivity and
campaign fetishization has been carefully exploited
by Republican strategists for political advantage.

News is what somebody somewhere wants to suppress;
all the rest is advertising.

—Alfred Harmsworth, 1st Viscount Northcliffe,

early-twentieth-century British press magnate

One of the most powerful metanarratives shaping Republican psychology—and Republican success—during the last several decades has been the party's unshakable belief, a belief amounting to religious faith, that a just and final victory over hated liberalism is almost within reach. According to this view, the majority of real Americans are innately conservative, and the only serious obstacle to reaching the promised land of permanent power lies in an all-powerful and diabolical liberal media conspiracy.* This conspiracy suppresses, misreports, or distorts all the

---

* A CBS News radio report on December 3, 2011, announcing Herman
  Cain's suspension of his presidential campaign was revealing. Every Cain

good things GOP candidates and officeholders are doing, and brainwashes the naturally conservative majority of the country into not seeing its own interests.

There is considerable psychological value in holding this view, because it reinforces the true believer's conviction that his ideology is sound and just, and the reason his political beliefs have not triumphed is that dark and sinister forces oppose them. This mental mechanism is an escape hatch for unwelcome facts and evidence that would otherwise undermine the faith of the follower: Should his favorite candidate or conservative hero commit a serious gaffe or become enmeshed in a scandal, he can rationalize the negative information by saying to himself that it is all a plot by the media to make conservatives look bad. Sometimes Republican candidates rise in the estimation of Republican primary voters in the wake of a scandal, as we saw with Newt in South Carolina, because being attacked by the liberal media octopus is a sure sign that you are on the right side.

And yet, at least since 1988, when Rush Limbaugh began his radio program, the Republican base has been developing its own comprehensive and interlocking media empire that operates on a separate and parallel track from the rest of the press. Except, that is, when its outpourings become sufficiently newsworthy or bizarre—think of the so-called war on Christmas—to arouse surprised comment in the wider world. For all their boo-hooing and defensiveness about the media, Republican operatives have created an impressive public relations industry in the form of talk radio, Fox News and its extended empire, the media outlets of fundamentalist churches such as Pat Robertson's *700 Club*, and other sympathetic

supporter the network interviewed suggested that Cain's troubles were exclusively the fault of the media.

if somewhat more outlandish affiliates such as those of Sun Myung Moon* and Richard Mellon Scaife. This media powerhouse has become an enormous cultural force, or more properly, an enormous countercultural force, with a mass following and staying power greater than the original counterculture of the 1960s.

This right-wing media powerhouse has created its own reality in order to bamboozle the gullible. On AM radio, which is totally dominated by right-wing personalities such as Limbaugh, Sean Hannity, and the rest of their tribe, insignificant issues that normal people would otherwise hardly waste their time thinking about assume the dimensions of all-encompassing conspiracies: ACORN (Association of Community Organizations for Reform Now), the New Black Panther Party, or Saul Alinsky.† This sort of thing is not unknown in our history: In the 1930s, the radio ranting of Father Coughlin had a substantial national listenership. But it is a little disconcerting that almost no one in the Republican Party will ever cross Limbaugh, even when he steps way beyond the bounds of decency—and those few who have done so have usually had to issue cringing apologies.

Should any outlet of the national media not within the orbit of reliably conservative ownership write a negative story about some aspect of the Republican agenda or Republican personalities, the media bias cry will arise. The chief demons are the *New York Times* and the *Washington Post*, and this despite their employing conserva-

---

* Korean billionaire Sun Myung Moon is the leader and chief deity of the Unification Church religious cult and owner of the *Washington Times*. The standing Beltway joke is that, whereas the *Washington Post* is the CIA's paper, the *Washington Times* is the KCIA's paper.

† Chicago-based political activist Saul Alinsky would have a difficult time conspiring about anything, since he has been dead for forty years. Yet it is a catechism of the lunatic right that Alinsky was a major influence on Barack Obama, who was ten years old when Alinsky passed away. "Saul Alinsky radicalism is at the heart of Obama," according to Newt Gingrich.

tive columnists such as George Will, Charles Krauthammer, Michael Gerson, Jennifer Rubin, Kathleen Parker, Ross Douthat, and David Brooks, among others. The GOP's belief in an implacably hostile anti-Republican bias persists despite both papers having enthusiastically trumpeted the false premises of the invasion of Iraq. In the last year or two, the *Post* has begun sounding like the Murdoch-subsidized *Weekly Standard* in its editorials bemoaning the possibility of even modest reductions to a Pentagon budget that has doubled in a decade, and in its strident advocacy of an Iran policy that risks all-out war.

There is a stark contrast between a vigorous, popular, and well-financed right-wing press always on the offensive about some issue or other and a diffident, sniffish, and out-of-touch mainstream press that is losing circulation and viewership despite hiring ever more explicitly ideological and controversial writers for its op-ed pages. This contrast defines the present media landscape. It is less the explicit flaws of each camp but rather the interactions between them that contribute to civic malaise and dysfunction in America. The right-wing media aggressively attempt to set the national news agenda through ever more prurient scoops—a technique pioneered by Matt Drudge in the mid-1990s—and the mainstream press, which, after ignoring the scoops for a while, reacts timidly and hesitantly, and settles on a middle-of-the-road stance that satisfies nobody and drives away readership.

Ever since the bifurcation of electronic media into a more or less respectable hard news segment and a rabidly ideological talk radio and politically propagandistic cable TV arm, the "respectable" media have been terrified of any criticism for perceived bias. Hence, they hew to the practice of false evenhandedness. Paul Krugman has skewered this tactic as a centrist cop-out. "I joked long ago," he wrote in one of his columns, "that if one party declared that the earth was flat, the headlines would read 'Views Differ on Shape of Planet.'"[1] This sort of faux objectivity has gone so far that the *New York Times*'s current public editor, Arthur Brisbane, wrote a column naïvely asking readers whether his paper should print the truth if a public figure lied.[2]

The constant drizzle of "there the two parties go again!" stories combines with the hazy confusion of poorly informed voters to help Republicans reap electoral dividends. The United States has nearly the lowest voter participation among all the Western democracies. This is at least in part a consequence of the decline of trust in government institutions, a condition that Republicans have shrewdly exacerbated. If government is a racket, and both parties are the same, why vote? And if the uninvolved middle declines to vote, the net result is to increase the electoral clout of a more dedicated minority that is daily being whipped into a lather by three hours of Rush Limbaugh or Fox News.

Economic trends have exacerbated the prevailing drift toward ever more pervasive, and ever shallower, coverage. At one time the big metropolitan newspapers were reliable cash machines that could afford in-depth reporting. But intoxicated by the financialization of the economy, newspaper owners were not satisfied with annual profits of only 10 percent. They had to be closer to 20 percent. So they made little serious reinvestment in the core business while responding tardily and ineffectively to the digitization of media. Some owners just looted their papers, as Sam Zell did to the *Chicago Tribune*. The last five years have seen a series of failures of once venerable newspapers and magazines from coast to coast. And those who have survived have seen their newsrooms gutted and pages slashed, and foreign bureaus have been closed around the world.

Political coverage in our nation's capital suffers from its own peculiar defects. Washington, D.C., is not a true metropolitan capital, like London or Paris. It is in reality a company town possessing little business activity other than retail, which must exist in any city, that is not directly or indirectly tied to the presence of the federal government. The expanding metropolis has crawled almost to the foothills of the Blue Ridge Mountains in the last thirty years. During my career, the Dulles corridor transformed from a rural vista between the Washington Beltway and the city's international airport into a *Futurama* landscape, where office blocks have sprouted like mushrooms. These structures house military contractors, homeland security profiteers, or information technology outfits hawking their wares to the government at a 400 percent markup. You will look in vain for a steel mill, a foundry, or an auto parts plant. Washington is a company town just as Homestead, Pennsylvania, was in the days of Andrew Carnegie, but in this case the company's product is politics (and military hardware). In a company town, everybody knows everybody else's business. The politicians and their consultants and fixers are well known to the lobbyists, contractors, and entrepreneurs.

The press fits comfortably into this incestuous ecosystem. Gone are the days of old-fashioned beat reporters who slowly worked their way up by breaking stories and ferreting out real news. Rather, more and more the establishment journalists come with journalism degrees from places like Columbia, and their "scoops" have been deliberately leaked; their outlooks evolve naturally to accommodate the attitudes of the oversized village they are reporting on.

It is probably difficult to identify with the predicament of an unemployed sheet-metal worker in Niles, Ohio, when you have reached the exalted station in your profession that results in an invitation to the annual White House Correspondents' Association Dinner. By no coincidence, the guest list includes a large number of Hollywood personalities, whom the establishment press corps increasingly resembles. It is hard to evaluate the evening: Is the press having its fun at the politicians' expense, seeing the Leader of the Free World hamming it up on stage like a Borscht Belt comedian? Or are the politicians putting one over on reporters by co-opting them into a performance that plays on the media's vanity and social-climbing instincts as it blunts their objectivity? The vulgarity of George W. Bush's turning his Iraq policy into a parody skit, with the press corps yukking it up over his search for Saddam's purported weapons of mass destruction under his Oval Office desk, gives one pause. It is all a bit like the antics at Bohemian Grove or an initiation ceremony of Skull and Bones: the elite of our country at play. The late George Carlin's words sum up what the Washington correspondents' dinner says to the public at large: "It's a club, and you ain't in it!"

This incestuousness helps explain why the major media often break their own rules when reporting on politics. Usually, when writing about local news, human interest features, and the like, the papers fully identify the average Joe who happens to have witnessed the car crash in question or come down with the disease of the month. But the higher up one goes, and the greater the political importance of the story, the less likely the Washington media are to identify a source by name, even when (or, rather, *particularly* when) the source is putting out self-serving spin to advance the agenda of the administration, agency, or party for which he or she works.

The *Washington Post*, the hometown newsletter of the Beltway elite, is particularly egregious in this respect. From time to time its ombudsman writes a high-minded column about how the *Post* has strict internal guidelines on the use of anonymous sources. But over and over again one can pick up the paper and see front-page stories laden with phrases like "according to senior White House officials," "according to sources close to the president," "according to a source requesting anonymity because he is not authorized to speak on the matter," and my favorite, "according to an official familiar with the president's thinking." Was that the White House psychiatrist, or maybe the first lady? In the great majority of cases these sources are blowing their organization's horn and advancing its agenda, either by praising their own policy or attacking their opponent's. Or they are launching a political trial balloon to see what the popular response will be. These people are not whistle-blowers, so why do they require the cloak of anonymity—and why does the press grant it to them?

One can understand why members of a presidential administration seek anonymity. They are still promoting their political agenda, but they are doing so by leaking classified information. Ordinarily, it is not illegal for a reporter to receive classified information (although some administrations, angered by the kind of leaks they don't like, have considered using the 1917 Espionage Act to attempt to prosecute reporters). What is clearly illegal is for a duly cleared federal employee to divulge such information.

Presidential administrations always leak like sieves. As the Beltway saying has it, "The ship of state is the only vessel that leaks from the top." But during the 2002 and 2003 run-up to the Iraq invasion, the flow of secrets became a geyser. Leaking information that could compromise sources and methods of collection is a serious matter; electronic intelligence data in particular is highly sensitive and divulging it is punished with draconian severity. Yet somehow that didn't matter when the objective was to provide a pretext for the war.

The deeper injury that the run-up to the Iraq war caused to our national security—and we shall only know the complete story in the fullness of time—lay in the flood of clues about the U.S. intelligence operations recklessly revealed by the Bush administration during its advertising blitz. The official conclusions that justified the pretext for the war were of course nonsense. But a competent foreign intelligence service might have connected the dots among the hundreds of publicly disclosed data points to compromise the sources and methods used by our intelligence agencies.

Most people now know the disgraceful story of the selling of the Iraq invasion: how a president and his advisers spun the pretext to the public through the willing agency of the news media, and how it led to a trillion-dollar strategic disaster. Less appreciated is the more subtle long-term damage this public relations stunt may have done to U.S. national security. The successful campaign to spin the media— and most of the media rushed to set aside their own professionalism in a desire to be spun—was accompanied by unprecedented pressure on intelligence analysts to come up with something, anything, no matter how threadbare the evidence, in order to feed the media. It was a milepost in the systematic politicization of U.S. intelligence agencies. Intelligence officers got the message: Get with the program. You no longer inform the policy making; your job is to lend a veneer of plausibility to a marketing campaign for a course already determined by politicians and their campaign advisers.

And it *was* a marketing campaign. As Andrew Card, chief of staff to President Bush, disclosed in an unguarded moment when asked about the timing of the war, "From a marketing point of view, you don't introduce new products in August." The decision to go to war was a product for the administration to sell, like laundry detergent. And the media happily complied, and ran the advocacy campaign as if it were a sponsored ad. In their gullibility, however, the press failed to consider that they weren't even being paid, as they would have been if Procter & Gamble had purchased a thirty-second spot or a full-page ad.

It was about that time, in mid-2002, that I began to turn to the online editions of the overseas press: Britain's *Guardian* or *Financial Times*, or Germany's *Der Spiegel*. It is a sad commentary on the U.S. news media—commonly believed to be operating in the freest country in the world, with explicit constitutional protections, no prior restraint on publishing, and generally much laxer libel laws—that the foreign press could write more balanced and accurate reports on a major political decision by the U.S. government than the bulk of our domestic media. The Knight-Ridder chain of newspapers (now McClatchy) was an honorable exception, as it generally showed a proper degree of skepticism about U.S. government claims.

According to a 2012 evaluation by Reporters Without Borders, the United States' press ranks as only the forty-seventh freest in the world.[3] One of the criteria the organization used to determine its ranking was whether the press in a given country practiced self-censorship, regardless of the formal legal protection it might enjoy (the United States ranked particularly poorly in the 2012 report, sliding twenty-seven places from the previous evaluation, because so many reporters had been arrested covering Occupy Wall Street protests).

☆

The mainstream media's toxic symbiosis with our two entrenched parties and the permanent shadow government have made it difficult for the average American to assemble an accurate and coherent picture of the world, much less make informed judgments about our foreign and national security policies or understand how America is perceived abroad. Rather than strive to be objective, our media personalities have become unofficial government representatives, particularly when foreign and national security policy are concerned. And when the war drums are beating, they are more like cheerleaders than objective reporters.

Tom Friedman, the *New York Times*'s wunderkind and resident Deep Thinker on globalization, is a marquee example of this syndrome. In the run-up to the Iraq invasion, Friedman acted with all the restraint and objectivity of the World War II *Why We Fight* series, albeit with fewer facts. Here he is in an interview justifying the invasion of Iraq, using the standard tough-guy language of the coddled and comfortable who never experience combat.

> What they needed to see was American boys and girls going house to house, from Basra to Baghdad, um, and basically saying, "Which part of this sentence don't you understand?" You don't think, you know, we care about our open society, you think this bubble fantasy, we're just gonna to let it grow? Well, Suck. On. This. . . . We could have hit Saudi Arabia. It was part of that bubble. Could have hit Pakistan. We hit Iraq because we could. That's the real truth.

Likewise, here he is in another interview, justifying U.S. policy in the face of a growing insurgency:

> [A]nd sometimes it takes a two-by-four across the side of the head to get that message.

All very edifying, but when the occupation of Iraq began to stretch into years, Friedman adopted a new leitmotif: Bush had screwed up the postinvasion administration of the country. Still, Friedman flailed about for the next several years, offering one scheme after another to rescue the warmongering policy he had so recklessly promoted before finally recommending disengagement. He did not have the sense, or perhaps the intellectual honesty, to admit that all the bad consequences of the occupation, including torture and ethnic cleansing, were the fruit of a poisoned tree. Or, in the words of former Supreme Court justice Robert Jackson, that making an unprovoked military attack is "the supreme international crime," differing from others only in that it encompasses all of the evil that follows. Yet Friedman is still pontificating from his platform at the *New York Times*, where, unchastened, he is now venting his belligerence against another Middle Eastern country: Having dispensed with Iraq, he has now turned to Iran.

Even now, almost a decade after the invasion, when the malign consequences of the military intervention have become clear—the false pretenses for the attack, the inordinate financial and human cost, the weakening of America's strategic and moral positions in the world—the establishment press is adopting a see-no-evil approach. Jon Meacham, formerly *Newsweek*'s resident intellectual, recently became a dispenser of etiquette rules for dealing with embarrassing subjects like the war. On a television talk show, he upbraided a guest for suggesting that President Bush had lied the country into war. At issue was less the facts at hand; to Meacham, sounding like Miss Manners, it was a question of civility: "To say someone lied adds a corrosive element to the public dialogue that we just don't need."[4] For self-appointed custodians of the public good, it is a lesser sin for American politicians to lie than for someone to call them out for lying.

Worse yet is Bill Kristol, who began his career as a partisan attack dog, became editor of the Murdoch-subsidized *Weekly Standard*, and graduated to a brief stint on the Platonic throne of the *New York Times* op-ed page. There are only two things that characterize his otherwise uninteresting persona: He is in favor of war in every conceivable circumstance, and he is always wrong. He is almost a reverse barometer for evaluating events. Yet he got on the payroll of the Gray Lady in 2008 for a one-year run, a dispenser of interpretations of the news at America's prestige paper. The examples can be multiplied. The salient problem is not that they are partisan enthusiasts (the Democrats have plenty of their own people polluting the op-ed pages with their versions of the party line), but that they are so consistently wrong, and yet they are never called to account for being wrong.

Michael Gerson was George W. Bush's speechwriter at the time of the Iraq invasion. He helped fashion Bush's second inaugural address, which contained the almost apocalyptic message that America's avenging sword would liberate a Middle East in chains. The key phrase in the address, "fire in the minds of men," derived from a book of the same name about nineteenth-century revolutionaries and anarchists.[5] It is fascinating that Gerson, writing for an erstwhile proponent of a humble foreign policy, inserted words in the president's mouth proclaiming a violent revolution in the manner of Trotsky. After his heady days as the Bakunin of the Bush Doctrine, Gerson is now dispensing snack-bar opinions in the *Washington Post* on the electability of Republican candidates, and similar mundane political fodder.

Although I have mainly discussed op-ed columnists,* the same syndrome applies to a lesser extent to reporters. The case of Judith Miller and her role in drumming up the Iraq war is too well known to need recapitulation here, but fellow *Times* reporter Michael Gordon continues to act as a faithful stenographer of whichever line the government happens to be promoting on national security and foreign "threats." Bob Woodward at the *Post*, with his "just so" stories

---

* Many of these pundits are former government speechwriters and press secretaries, i.e., propagandists rather than people with any deep policy expertise. Even that is a step up from most of the rest of the pundit class, who have no discernible professional qualifications whatever other than glibness, ambition, and a natural talent for mugging at the camera.

and improbable recall of dialogue he never heard, has served as a vehicle for senior White House personnel to dispense self-aggrandizing gossip. Some of my friends used to joke that you always knew whenever Colin Powell had an official position in Washington, because Woodward would come out with a book shortly thereafter.

Some of this bad reporting may be due to the reporter's ignorance of technical subject matter having to do with budgets or weapon systems. I recall getting a phone call late in the afternoon shortly after a B-1 bomber had crashed on a training flight. I was attempting to explain to ABC News reporter Bob Zelnick that the Air Force suspected that the cause of the crash was a fire resulting from a broken fuel line in the engine nacelle. "What's a nacelle?" was the testy and impatient response from the man who had been ABC News's chief Pentagon correspondent for eight years. With that kind of subject knowledge, no wonder government spokespeople can snow the press.

Just as preadolescent boys are fascinated by secret decoder rings, the Washington media reporting on national security issues are thrilled by being in the loop about important decisions before the public hears about them. This includes being privy to classified information. Now it is true that the publication of some classified intelligence could be severely damaging to the country's security, but most of the millions of classified documents that the government generates every year are prosaic, low-level stuff whose content any reasonably well-informed person could infer. A small percentage of classified material is information of no real national security importance but whose revelation would be politically embarrassing. But who is and who is not in the loop for getting all these intelligence tidbits in Washington, the ultimate company town, is a big deal that top-level officials exploit.

More interesting than the content of classified material is how it is used politically. The rules of declassification—there are lots of rules, but they are incoherent and contradictory—are used so arbitrarily that classified material more often becomes a means of baiting the press to advance a political agenda. Did Bradley Manning, the U.S. Army enlisted man who gave thousands of pages of sensitive government documents to the Web site WikiLeaks, damage national security? Perhaps he did, but no reasonable person with any experience in government should have taken the government at its word when it attempted to justify holding him without charge or legal counsel and in abusive conditions. Especially not when senior administration officials from both parties also leak classified information to the press to further their objectives. National security secrets have become degraded to the status of gossipy tidbits for the press. I am sure a Venn diagram of persons who want to boil Bradley Manning in oil would hardly intersect a diagram of persons who wanted similar treatment meted out to Scooter Libby for blowing the cover of a covert CIA officer—an extremely serious matter.

Just in case you think that the mainstream press learned its lesson from Iraq—about promoting the invasion of another country based on anonymous sources—we have this piece in the November 20, 2011, *Washington Post*: "Iran may have sent Libya shells for chemical weapons." And what are the documented sources for this scoop?

> U.S. officials said . . . several sources . . . [a] U.S. official with access to classified information . . . a third U.S. official said . . . [o]ne U.S. official said . . . another U.S. official said.[6]

Here we go again! Even after the complete discrediting of the pretext for the Iraq war, the mainstream media continue to follow the shopworn Iraq template in their reporting on Iran. Three months after that anonymous revelation about Iranian machinations in Libya, the *Post* was back at it with another front-page bombshell; this time Iran was doubling down, backing Assad's regime in Syria with weapons. How do we know this?

> "The aid from Iran is increasing, and is increasingly focused on lethal assistance," said one of the officials, insisting on anonymity to discuss intelligence reports from the region. . . . U.S. officials *declined to address allegations about specific acts.* But one of the officials who spoke on the condition of anonymity said intelligence agencies have documented reports of a wide range of assistance. [7] [emphasis mine]

No intelligent person ever doubted the brutality of the Assad regime. But the eagerness of our prestige media to tie Iran to events in Syria precisely at a time when the world is already on edge about Iran's purported nuclear capabilities—a subject far more nuanced and ambiguous than you would think from reading articles in our leading papers—demonstrates the danger to our country of a credulous and uncritical press. Liberals habitually work themselves into a lather about the antics of Rush Limbaugh or Glenn Beck, but they are really just political gargoyles looking for ratings as they whip up the GOP faithful. The true danger lies in an ostensibly neutral journalism that most Americans count on to tell them what is going on in the world but which too often acts as a stenographer for powerful and self-serving factions in government operating under a cloak of anonymity. These people have misled us in the past and will mislead us in the future if they are not vigorously challenged.

8

GIVE ME THAT
OLD-TIME RELIGION

**The religious right provides the foot soldiers for
the GOP. This fact has profound implications for the
rest of the Republicans' ideological agenda.**

★ ★ ★

Sin, sin, sin! You're all sinners!
You're all doomed to perdition!

—Burt Lancaster as Elmer Gantry (1960)

Having observed politics up close and personal for most of
my adult lifetime, I have come to the conclusion that the
rise of politicized religious fundamentalism may have
been the key ingredient in the transformation of the Republican
Party. Politicized religion provides a substrate of beliefs that
rationalizes—at least in the minds of its followers—all three of the
GOP's main tenets: wealth worship, war worship, and the permanent culture war.

Religious cranks ceased to be a minor public nuisance in this
country beginning in the 1970s and grew into a major element of
the Republican rank and file. Pat Robertson's strong showing in the
1988 Iowa presidential caucus signaled the gradual merger of politics and religion in the party. Unfortunately, at the time I mostly
underestimated the implications of what I was seeing. It did strike

me as oddly humorous that a fundamentalist staff member in my congressional office was going to take time off to convert the heathen in Greece, a country that had been overwhelmingly Christian for almost two thousand years. I recall another point, in the early 1990s, when a different fundamentalist GOP staffer said that dinosaur fossils were a hoax. As a mere legislative mechanic toiling away in what I held to be a civil rather than ecclesiastical calling, I did not yet see that ideological impulses far different from mine were poised to capture the party of Lincoln.

The results of this takeover are all around us: If the American people poll more like Iranians or Nigerians than Europeans or Canadians on questions of evolution, scriptural inerrancy, the presence of angels and demons, and so forth, it is due to the rise of the religious right, its insertion into the public sphere by the Republican Party, and the consequent normalizing of formerly reactionary beliefs. All around us now is a prevailing anti-intellectualism and hostility to science. Politicized religion is the sheet anchor of the dreary forty-year-old culture wars.

The Constitution notwithstanding, there is now a de facto religious test for the presidency: Major candidates are encouraged (or coerced) to share their feelings about their faith in a revelatory speech, or a televangelist like Rick Warren will dragoon the candidates (as he did with Obama and McCain in 2008) to debate the finer points of Christology, offering himself as the final arbiter. Half a century after John F. Kennedy put to rest the question of whether a candidate of a minority denomination could be president, the Republican Party has reignited the kinds of seventeenth-century religious controversies that advanced democracies are supposed to have outgrown. And some in the media seem to have internalized the GOP's premise that the religion of a candidate is a matter for public debate.

Throughout the 2012 Republican presidential campaign, Mitt Romney was dogged with questions about his religion. The spark was a hitherto obscure fundamentalist preacher from Texas, Robert Jeffress, who attacked Romney's Mormonism by doubting whether he could really be considered a Christian. The media promptly set aside the issues that should have been paramount— Romney's views on economic and foreign policy—in order to spend a week giving respectful consideration to an attention-grabbing rabble-rouser. They then proceeded to pester the other candidates with the loaded question of whether they thought Romney was a Christian. CNN's Candy Crowley was particularly egregious in this respect, pressing Herman Cain and Michele Bachmann for a response and becoming indignant when they refused to answer. The question did not deserve an answer, because Crowley had set it up to legitimate a false premise: that Romney's religious belief was a legitimate issue of public debate. This is a perfect example of how the media reinforce an informal but increasingly binding religious test for public office that the Constitution formally bans. Like the British constitution, the test is no less powerful for being unwritten.

The religious right's professed insistence upon "family values"* might appear at first blush to be at odds with the anything but saintly personal behavior of many of its leading proponents. Some of this may be due to the general inability of human beings to reflect on conflicting information: I have never ceased to be amazed at how facts manage to bounce off people's consciousness like pebbles

---

* "Morality" in this case usually boils down to ultraconventional prudery about private sexual behavior, the standards—but not practices—of which were established in Victorian England, and which eventually caused the comic uproar that led to the Clinton impeachment. Unfortunately, morality thus defined frequently ignores other aspects of ethics.

off armor plate. But there is another, uniquely religious aspect that also comes into play: the predilection of fundamentalist denominations to believe in practice, even if not entirely in theory, in the doctrine of "cheap grace," a derisive term coined by the theologian Dietrich Bonhoeffer. By that he meant the inclination of some religious adherents to believe that once they had been "saved," not only would all past sins be wiped away, but future ones, too—so one could pretty much behave as before. Cheap grace is a divine get-out-of-jail-free card. Hence the tendency of the religious base of the Republican Party to cut some slack for the peccadilloes of candidates who claim to have been washed in the blood of the Lamb and reborn to a new and more Christian life. The religious right is willing to overlook a politician's individual foibles, no matter how poor an example he or she may make, if they publicly identify with fundamentalist values. In 2011 the Family Research Council, the fundamentalist lobbying organization, gave Representative Joe Walsh of Illinois an award for "unwavering support of the family."[1] Representative Walsh's ex-wife might beg to differ, as she claims he owes her over one hundred thousand dollars in unpaid child support, a charge he denies.

Of course, the proper rituals must be observed before an erring politician can obtain absolution. In November 2011, at a forum sponsored by religious conservatives in Iowa, all of the GOP presidential candidates struck the expected notes of contrition and humility as they laid bare their souls before the assembled congregation (the event was held in a church). Most of them, including Cain, who was then still riding high, choked up when discussing some bleak midnight of their lives (he chose not to address the fresh sexual harassment charges against him, which surely would have qualified as a trying personal experience preying on his mind). Even the old reprobate Gingrich misted up over some contrived misdeed in-

tended to distract attention from his well-known adventures in se-
rial matrimony.

All of these gloomy obsequies of repentance having been observed, Gingrich gave a stirring example of why he is hands-down
the best extemporaneous demagogue in contemporary America.
Having purged his soul of all guilty transgressions, he turned his
attention to the far graver sins bedeviling the American nation.

> If we look at history from the mid-1960s, we've gone from a
> request for toleration to an imposition of intolerance. We've
> gone from a request to understand others to a determination
> to close down those who hold traditional values. I think that
> we need to be very aggressive and very direct. The degree to
> which the left is prepared to impose intolerance and to drive
> out of existence traditional religion is a mortal threat to our
> civilization and deserves to be taken head-on and described
> as what it is, which is the use of government to repress the
> American people against their own values.

That is as good an example as any of cheap grace as practiced
by seasoned statesmen like Gingrich—a bid for redemption turned
on its head to provide a forum for one of the Republican Party's
favorite pastimes: taking opportunistic swipes at the dreaded liberal bogeyman. How quickly one forgets one's own moral lapses
when one can consider the manifold harms inflicted on our nation
by godless leftists!

★

The GOP's growing fascination with war is connected to the fundamentalist mind-set. The Old Testament abounds in tales of
slaughter—God orders the killing of Midianite male infants and

the enslavement of the balance of the population, and inspires the genocide of the Canaanites, the slaying of miscreants with the jaw-bone of an ass, and so on—and since American fundamentalists often seem to prefer the Old Testament to the New (particularly that portion of the New Testament known as the Sermon on the Mount), it is but a short step to approving war as a divinely inspired mission. This sort of thinking has led to such phenomena as the late televangelist Jerry Falwell once proclaiming that God was prowar.[2]

More disturbing, fundamentalist ministers have been influenc-ing the Republican Party's Middle East policies. A fundamentalist megachurch preacher from Texas, John Hagee, has made a belief in the "rapture" (a word found nowhere in the Bible) the centerpiece of his ministry; he believes it will be triggered by an apocalyptic battle at the end of the world, in the Middle East. He contorts the Bible to predict that Russia and various Islamic countries will invade Israel and be destroyed by God. This supernatural event in turn will cause the Antichrist, whom he identifies as the head of the European Union,* to engineer a confrontation over Israel between China and the United States. Hagee heads the lobbying group Christians United for Israel, and from this perch he routinely proposes that the United States adopt the most militaristic and confrontational poli-cies against the Islamic world, including a preemptive nuclear strike against Iran. It is not entirely by happenstance that the GOP candi-dates in 2012 have fallen over backward in an effort to appear ever more anti-Iran. In 2008, John McCain, not noted for public dis-plays of piety, eagerly sought and gratefully received Hagee's en-dorsement of his presidential candidacy—an endorsement McCain

---

* The current president of the European Commission, the executive body of the European Union, is a gentleman named José Manuel Durão Barroso. Who knew?

later rejected after some bizarre remarks surfaced that Hagee had made about Hitler and the Jews.

★

The apocalyptic frame of reference of fundamentalists like Hagee, their belief in an imminent Armageddon, psychologically conditions them to steer the country into conflict, not only on foreign fields (some evangelicals thought Saddam was the Antichrist and therefore a suitable target for cruise missiles), but also in the realm of domestic political controversy. Compromise is a dirty word if you are doing God's bidding. It is thus perhaps hardly surprising that the most adamant proponent of the view that there was no debt-ceiling problem was Michele Bachmann, the darling of the fundamentalist right. What does it matter, anyway, if the country defaults? We shall presently abide in the bosom of the Lord.

If the world is divided between the Children of Light and the Children of Darkness, then compromise in the spirit of traditional representative government becomes difficult. As a veteran of many late-night legislative sessions, I can personally attest to the fact that achieving legislation that will pass both houses of Congress is sometimes a grubby business, like sausage making, but the practical alternatives are either anarchy or dictatorship. As deal makers like Howard Baker or Bob Dole have given way to ideological purists infused with their own sense of godly virtue, such as Rick Santorum and Bachmann, it is hardly a wonder that the GOP has become the party of no.

When those professing this kind of religious dogmatism get involved in making foreign policy, the results can be disastrous. The Israeli newspaper *Haaretz* reported that George Bush allegedly told Palestinian prime minister Mahmoud Abbas, in a meeting about Middle East peace in 2003, "God told me to strike at al Qaeda and I struck them, and then he instructed me to strike at Saddam, which I did, and now I am determined to solve the problem in the Middle East."[3] We have come a long way from the legacy of Eisenhower and Marshall if our leaders are thinking about the intractable crises of the Middle East in that fashion.

★

Some liberal writers have opined that the socioeconomic gulf separating the business wing of the GOP and the religious right make it an unstable coalition that could crack. I am not so sure. There is no basic disagreement on which direction the two factions want to take the country, merely how far it should go. The plutocrats would drag us back to the Gilded Age; the theocrats to the Salem witch trials. If anything, the two groups are increasingly beginning to resemble each other. Many televangelists have espoused what has come to be known as the prosperity gospel—the health-and-wealth/name-it-and-claim-it gospel of economic entitlement. If you are wealthy, it is a sign of God's favor. If not, too bad! This rationale may explain why some poor voters will defend the prerogatives of billionaires. In any case, at the beginning of the 2012 presidential cycle, those consummate plutocrats the Koch brothers pumped money into Bachmann's campaign, so one should probably not make too much of a potential plutocrat-theocrat split.[4]

Most of the religious enthusiasts I observed during my tenure on the Hill seemed to have little reluctance to mix God and Mammon. Rick Santorum did not blink at legislative schemes to pay off his campaign contributors: In 2005 he introduced a bill to forbid the National Weather Service from providing weather forecasts for free that commercial forecasters—like AccuWeather, a Pennsylvania-based company which had contributed to his campaign—wanted to charge for. Tom DeLay's purported concern about the dignity and sanctity of human life, touchingly on display during the controversy over whether Terri Schiavo's husband had the right to tell doctors to remove her feeding tube after seeing her comatose for fifteen years, could always be qualified by strategic infusions of campaign cash. DeLay's quashing of bills to prohibit serious labor abuses demonstrates that even religious virtue can be flexible when there are campaign donations involved.

One might imagine that the religious right's agenda would be incompatible with the concerns for privacy and individual autonomy by those who consider themselves to belong to the libertarian wing of the Republican Party—the "don't tread on me," "live free or die" crowd that Grover Norquist once called the "leave me alone" conservatives. Given their profound distaste for an oppressive and intrusive federal government, one would think they might have trepidations about a religious movement determined to impose statutory controls on private behavior that libertarians nominally hold to be nobody's business, and particularly not the government's business.

Some more libertarian-leaning Republicans have in fact pushed back against the religious right. Former House majority leader Dick Armey expressed his profound distaste for the tactics of the religious right in 2006—from the safety of the sidelines—by blasting its leadership in unequivocal terms:

> [James] Dobson and his gang of thugs are real nasty bullies. I pray devoutly every day, but being a Christian is no excuse for being stupid. There's a high demagoguery coefficient to issues like prayer in schools. Demagoguery doesn't work unless it's dumb, shallow as water on a plate. These issues are easy for the intellectually lazy and can appeal to a large de-

mographic. These issues become bigger than life, largely because they're easy. There ain't no thinking.[5]

Armey had previously been an economics professor at several cow colleges in Texas, and when he came to Congress in 1985, libertarian economics was his forte. I do not recall religious issues motivating his political ideology; instead, economics was what gripped him, particularly the flat tax, which he tirelessly promoted. I believe his departure from Congress was impelled not only by the fact that he was not on the inside track to become Speaker, but also because of his disillusionment with the culture wars, as his passionate denunciation of Dobson suggests. But later, Barack Obama's election and the rise of the Tea Party induced a miraculous change of heart in Armey, as no doubt did the need to raise money for his lobbying organization, known as FreedomWorks. By 2009, Armey had become a significant voice of the Tea Party. As such, he attempted to declare a truce between fiscal and social conservatives, who would thenceforth bury their squabbles and concentrate on dethroning the Kenyan usurper in the Oval Office. That meant soft-pedaling social issues that might alarm fiscally conservative but socially moderate voters, particularly women, who lived in the wealthier suburbs.

In September 2010 Armey took one step further in his reconciliation with the people he had called thugs and bullies when he announced that a GOP majority in Congress would again take up the abortion fight, which was only right and proper for those who held such a sincere moral conviction.[6] When the Republicans duly won the House two months later, they did precisely that. State legislatures across the country followed suit: Ohio, Texas, and Virginia enacted the most severe abortion restrictions in any legislative session in memory. Suddenly Armey didn't seem to have any problem with social issues preempting his economic agenda.

The Tea Party, which initially described itself as wholly concerned with debt, deficit, and federal overreach, gradually unmasked itself as being almost as theocratic as the activists from the religious right that Armey had denounced only a few years before. If anything, they were even slightly more disposed than the rest of the Republican Party to inject religious issues into the political realm. According to an academic study of the Tea Party, "[T]hey seek 'deeply religious' elected officials, approve of religious leaders' engaging in politics and want religion brought into political debates."[7] The Tea Party faithful are not so much libertarian as authoritarian, the furthest thing from a "live free or die" constitutionalist.

Within the GOP libertarianism is a throwaway doctrine that is rhetorically useful in certain situations but often interferes with their core, more authoritarian, beliefs. When the two precepts collide, the authoritarian reflex prevails. In 2009 it was politically useful for the GOP to present the Tea Party as independent-leaning libertarians, when in reality the group was overwhelmingly Republican, with a high quotient of GOP activists and adherents of views common among the religious right. According to a 2010 Gallup poll, eight in ten Tea Party members identify themselves as Republicans.[8] Another study found that over half identified as members of the religious right and 55 percent of Tea Partiers agree that "America has always been and is currently a Christian nation"—6 points more than even the percentage of self-described Christian conservatives who would agree to that.[9] This religious orientation should have been evident from the brouhaha that erupted in mid-2009 over the charge that the Obama administration's new health-care reform plan would set up "death panels." While there was plenty to criticize about the health-care bill, the completely bogus charge garnered disproportionate attention. Republican political consultants immediately recognized that they had found a classic emotional issue that would resonate with the same people on the religious right who had been stirred up over the Terri Schiavo case.* The Tea Party, a supposedly independent group of fiscal conservatives outraged by Obama's profligate spending plans, fell prey to the hysteria Republican Party operatives whipped up over end-of-life counseling.[10] This self-unmasking of the Tea Party may help explain why, after three years in existence, public support for the organization has been dropping precipitously.[11]

Ayn Rand, an occasional darling of the Tea Party, has become a cult figure within the GOP in recent years. It is easy enough to see how her tough-guy, every-man-for-himself posturing would be a natural fit with the Wall Street bankers and the right-wing politicians they fund—notwithstanding the bankers' fondness for government bailouts. But Rand's philosophy found most of its adherents in the libertarian wing of the party, a group that overlaps with, but is certainly not identical to, the "business conservatives" who fund the bulk of the GOP's activities. There has always been a strong strain of rugged individualism in America, and the GOP has cleverly managed to co-opt that spirit to its advantage. The problem is that Rand proclaimed at every opportunity that she was a militant atheist who felt nothing but contempt for Christianity as a religion of weaklings possessing a slave mentality. So how do Republican candidates manage to bamboozle what is perhaps the largest single bloc in their voting base, the religious fundamentalists, about this? Certainly the ignorance of many fundamentalist values voters about the wider world and the life of the mind goes some distance toward explaining the paradox: GOP candidates

---

* Surveys have found a positive correlation between the fear of death and the intensity of religious motivation. See, e.g., Ya-Hui Wen, "Religiosity and Death Anxiety," *Journal of Human Resources and Adult Learning*, December 2010.

who enthuse over Rand at the same time as they thump their Bibles never have to explain this stark contradiction because most of their audience is blissfully unaware of who Ayn Rand was and what she advocated.* But voters can to some extent be forgiven their ignorance, because politicians have grown so skillful at misdirecting them about their intentions.[12]

This camouflaging of intentions is as much a strategy of the religious right and its leaders—James Dobson, Tony Perkins, Pat Robertson, and the rest—as it is of the GOP's more secular political leaders in Washington. After the debacle of the Schiavo case and the electoral loss in 2008, the religious right pulled back and regrouped. They knew that the full-bore, "theoconservative" agenda would not sell with a majority of voters. This strategy accounts for Robertson, founder of the Christian Coalition (who famously said that God sent a hurricane to New Orleans to punish the sodomites), stating the following in October 2011: "Those people in the Republican primary have got to lay off of this stuff. They're forcing their leaders, the front-runners, into positions that will mean they lose the general election." I doubt he thought the candidates held positions that were too extreme, merely that they should keep quiet about those positions until they had won the election. Max Blumenthal, author of *Republican Gomorrah*, argues that this is a "lying for Jesus" strategy that fundamentalists often adopt when dealing with the snares of a wicked and Godless world. Since Satan is the father of lies, one can be forgiven for fighting lies with lies.

Hence the policies pursued for at least two decades by the reli-

---

* Nearly two decades ago, Mark A. Noll, a professor of theology at Wheaton College and himself an evangelical, wrote *The Scandal of the Evangelical Mind* about the decline of intellectual pursuits among evangelicals.

gious right on the federal, state, and local levels. It usually starts at the school board, after some contrived uproar over sex education or liberal indoctrination. The stealthily fundamentalist school board candidates pledge to clean up the mess and "get back to basics." After a few years they capture a majority on the board, and suddenly *Catcher in the Rye* is heaved out of the curriculum and science teachers are under pressure to teach the (imaginary) controversy about evolutionary biology. This was the path to greater glory of Michele Bachmann: Her first run for public office, barely a dozen years ago, was for a seat on the school board in Stillwater, Minnesota. Up until then she had drawn a taxpayer-funded salary for five years working as an attorney for the Internal Revenue Service, not, of course, because she was one of those lazy, good-for-nothing government bureaucrats that Republican candidates routinely denounce. She was secretly studying the ways of the government beast so as to defeat it later on.

Bachmann, Rick Perry, and numerous other serving representatives and senators have all had ties to Christian Dominionism, a doctrine proclaiming that Christians are destined to dominate American politics and establish a new imperium resembling theocratic government. According to one profile of Perry, adherents of Dominionism "believe Christians—certain Christians—are destined to not just take 'dominion' over government, but stealthily climb to the commanding heights of what they term the 'Seven Mountains' of society, including the media and the arts and entertainment world."[13] Note the qualifier: "stealthily."

At the same religious forum where the GOP candidates confessed their sins, Bachmann went so far as to suggest that organized religion should keep its traditional legal privilege of tax exemption while being permitted to endorse political candidates from the pulpit.[14] The fact that government prohibits express political advocacy is in her imagination muzzling preachers rather than just being a quid pro quo for tax-exempt status equivalent to that imposed on any 501(c)3 or 501(c)4 nonprofit organization. But for Bachmann and others of like mind, this is persecution of a kind that fuels their sense of victimhood and righteous indignation.

It is not difficult to find examples in everyday life of acquaintances and associates whose ever-present sense of persecution is nothing more than a rationalization of their own anger and hostility. According to Canadian psychologist Robert Altemeyer, who has written extensively about the characteristics of the authoritarian personality, fundamentalists exhibit a high quotient of authoritarian traits:

> They are highly submissive to established authority, aggressive in the name of that authority, and conventional to the point of insisting everyone should behave as their authorities decide. They are fearful and self-righteous and have a lot of hostility in them that they readily direct toward various out-groups. They are easily incited, easily led, rather uninclined to think for themselves, largely impervious to facts and reason, and rely instead on social support to maintain their beliefs. They bring strong loyalty to their in-groups, have thick-walled, highly compartmentalized minds, use a lot of double standards in their judgments, are surprisingly unprincipled at times, and are often hypocrites.[15]

The history of Europe has largely been a history of religious wars, intolerance, and oppression: Government has been wielded countless times as the instrument and vindicator of divine truth. With the decline of formal religious belief after the senseless carnage of World War I, the aggressive and authoritarian ideologies of the early twentieth century filled the psychological need that state-controlled religion had previously supplied. Their doctrines were often just badly distorted religious dogma and attracted the same sort of true believer who needed an outlet for his free-floating hostility. There will always be a large number of people who crave certainty in an uncertain world.

The United States has been fortunate to have avoided some of the worst aspects of Europe's history. Luck had something to do with it, but so did a system of governance that permitted and encouraged religious pluralism. What America did not do was mandate a religious test for office or base its foreign or domestic policies on someone's tendentious reading of the Bible. If this country ever fully uncorks the genie of politicized religion, as the Republican Party has been attempting to do, we shall long regret it.

9

NO EGGHEADS WANTED

Consistent both with its strong base of support among fundamentalists and with its authoritarian belief structure, the GOP is increasingly anti-intellectual and antiscience.

☆ ☆ ☆

It is ironic that the United States should have been founded by intellectuals, for throughout most of our political history, the intellectual has been for the most part either an outsider, a servant or a scapegoat.

—Richard Hofstadter, *Anti-Intellectualism in American Life* (1964)

Fifty years ago, when he wrote his seminal book on the periodic waves of anti-intellectualism in America, Richard Hofstadter was highly critical of his own time. In retrospect, he was writing in a golden age of enlightenment. For it was also fifty years ago that, when a handful of kooks in the John Birch Society condemned the fluoridation of water as a communist conspiracy, the vast majority of the American people dismissed them as a fringe nuisance. The plot device of the popular movie *Dr. Strangelove* hinged on the actions of an antifluoridation fanatic, and everybody was in on the joke. But in 2011, a majority of the majority party of the United States House of Representatives voted against new consumer energy standards, arguing, among other things, that compact fluorescent lightbulbs were a radical leftist conspiracy. How did we ever get here?

The problem is unfortunately not new. In 1922, not long before the Scopes Monkey Trial, Woodrow Wilson told an interviewer who asked him for his views on evolution by natural selection, "Of course, like every other man of intelligence and education I do believe in organic evolution. It surprises me that at this late date such questions should be raised." And yet, ninety years later, after the genetic engineering of crops, the Human Genome Project, the discovery of evolving antibiotic-resistant bacteria, and innumerable other evidence of the evolution of organisms, such questions are not only raised, they have become a political litmus test on the right. The wise candidate ducks the issue, while the unscrupulous one panders to the uninformed.

Whether it is Michele Bachmann announcing that the HPV vaccine causes mental retardation, or Senator James Inhofe condemning the findings of climate scientists as a "hoax," or Rick Santorum doubting the validity of evolutionary biology, there can be no question that the GOP has placed itself squarely in the camp of the flat-earthers. This is a sad legacy for a previously forward-looking party, one that established public land-grant universities under President Lincoln and created science scholarships under President Eisenhower.

In 1957, when the Soviets launched *Sputnik*, American politicians wanted to hit the panic button. What this meant in cold war terms was to throw money at the Department of Defense and initiate crash programs to develop more and better weaponry. But President Eisenhower, having already cut military spending after the Korean War (and, as a result, balanced the budget), was loath to spend that kind of money. In any case, he knew but could not reveal to the public that there were classified programs on the drawing board that in time would redress any perceived disparity with the Soviets.

Instead, Ike proposed federal assistance to public education to improve the teaching of science and engineering, as well as scholarships to promising students. In his speeches at the time he emphasized that his science advisers had told him that the education of scientists and engineers was the highest national defense priority, *a higher priority than producing weapons.* Many of these newly minted scientists and engineers would, of course, work for the Department of Defense or NASA, but others would go on to infuse their skills into the civilian economy.

It was a shrewd argument to outflank the hawks, and a similar one to the way, a year prior to his science announcement, he had sold his idea for an interstate highway system. He knew that the nation's economic competitiveness would suffer from the antiquated roads of the 1950s, a system inferior to the autobahns he had seen in Germany at the end of World War II. To get his proposal through Congress he pitched it as the National Interstate and *Defense* Highways Act. Building a nation-spanning system of modern highways would, of course, require educating and training thousands of civil engineers.

But Eisenhower was not interested in raising up a generation of soulless technocrats. His vice president, Richard Nixon, gave an address that same year in which he emphasized the importance of teaching the humanities. Education had to be balanced: While they should establish a foundation in science, schools needed to educate the whole individual. He pledged that federal, state, and local governments would do whatever it took to make it happen, including raising teachers' salaries. Nixon's statement is an ironic counterpoint to the policies of today's Republican state governors and legislators, who appear to view schoolteachers as public enemy number one. In the 1950s and 1960s both parties could claim that their platforms embraced science and learning as national priorities. President Kennedy stressed the importance of education, and his White House guest lists were notable for having a high quotient of academics and intellectuals.

The first crack in the edifice of general political support for science and learning came in about 1970—incidentally, the same time that the economy started to transform, manufacturing started trickling out of the country, and the culture wars began. It started on the far left, where dissatisfaction with the Vietnam War found an outlet in a rejection of technology. The leftist antiwar crowd did not distinguish between the ethical and proper uses of technology and napalm. Some began to show distinct aspects of Ludditism—an ironic development, given that the forces of the left had been the advocates of science and "progress" ever since the French Revolution.

Thus, some of the sillier fringe theories of the seventies: mathematics as an arbitrary construct; schools of historical revisionism so focused on history's inevitable subjectivity that they questioned the existence of facts; and so on. This tendency reached its nadir in the brief fad of deconstructionism among the European left and a few academics in America. Beneath a lot of fake erudition, proponents argued (to the extent one could make any sense of it) that there was no stable reality at all, only arbitrary linguistic systems of power and oppression.

Most of the world laughed this leftist mumbo jumbo out of existence after a few years. It was a godsend to the growing conservative movement, however, to have such an object on the left to ridicule. Its main legacy is the phrase "political correctness," a term which has in most cases long outlived its usefulness but which right-wing talk radio continues to use incessantly as yet another weapon in its culture wars arsenal.

Anti-intellectualism as a mass phenomenon in contemporary American life arose gradually but steadily over the last thirty years, and it resides principally on the rightward end of the political spectrum. Its connection to the rise of the more extreme forms of religious fundamentalism, and their infection of the GOP's electoral base, is an obvious fact, but one which the mainstream media rarely brings up. Anti-intellectualism has been a recurring factor in American history since the country's founding; the difference between past episodes and the current situation, however, is both that it is now so closely identified with the fortunes of one of the two political parties and that it has deep institutional roots involving radio, TV, and print media as well as partisan "institutes," which generate slanted research on topics like evolution and climate change.

It is an enduring irony of history that Protestant Christianity arose as a religious reform movement among deeply learned scholars such as Luther, Calvin, and Zwingli. (By way of example, Luther's close collaborator Philipp Melanchthon studied philosophy, rhetoric, astronomy, Greek, law, mathematics, and medicine.) The reformed churches' insistence on discovering authentic religious texts, and their stress on the right and duty of all believers to be guided by their inner light on the basis of their own reading of these texts, fueled an impetus for greater popular literacy. But Protestantism's belief in scriptural inerrancy also led to offshoot denominations best characterized by doctrinal rigidity, hostility to artistic expression, and deep suspicion of intellectual activity that could undermine the accepted understanding of the revealed truth.

America has experienced periodic upwellings of evangelical

activism that have often spilled over into concrete political agendas. The Great Awakening of the early nineteenth century had variable results: It produced the Millerites, who predicted the end of the world would come on October 22, 1844, but also the movements for the abolition of slavery and women's suffrage. The anti–Wall Street populism that arose on the prairies in the late nineteenth century contained a strong element of evangelical activism. That insurgency did not quite succeed in overturning the two-party system or toppling the Wall Street barons, but it did spawn the progressive movement, which helped curb the prevailing political and economic abuses.

The evangelical insurgency of the late nineteenth and early twentieth centuries also produced the hideous excrescence of Prohibition, Comstock laws prohibiting the sale of novels by artists like Marcel Proust and James Joyce, and the all too familiar civil harassment of harmless personal behavior that seems to increase whenever zealots have the political whip hand. It was a sad capstone to a storied career that William Jennings Bryan, who stood up to the power of the money trust, championed the rights of labor, and opposed entry into the slaughter of World War I, should end his life in a Dayton, Tennessee, courtroom declaring that man is not a mammal. Perhaps he had been outraged by the Social Darwinists' perversion of Charles Darwin's scientific breakthrough. But he definitely signaled the opposition to science and intellectual life of a significant strain of American religious thought.

This strain lay mostly dormant in American political life from the 1920s until the last quarter of the twentieth century. In the meantime, a few conservatives attempted to breathe life into the notion that the movement should have a visible intellectual foundation. In the 1950s, conservatism was at a low ebb of intellectual

prestige. The liberal consensus was triumphant, and public intellectuals such as Lionel Trilling declared rather smugly:

> In the United States at this time Liberalism is not only the
> dominant but even the sole intellectual tradition. For it is the
> plain fact that nowadays there are no conservative or reaction-
> ary ideas in general circulation. This does not mean, of course,
> that there is no impulse to conservatism or to reaction. Such
> impulses are certainly very strong, perhaps even stronger than
> most of us know. But the conservative impulse and the reac-
> tionary impulse do not, with some isolated and some ecclesias-
> tical exceptions, express themselves in ideas but only in action
> or in irritable mental gestures which seek to resemble ideas.[1]

Soon those irritable mental gestures began to cloak themselves
in a fog of polysyllabic words. The mid-1950s marked the rise of a
more sophisticated brand of conservative, eager to dispense with
the crudities of Joe McCarthy accusing General George C. Marshall, the strategic architect of the U.S. victory in World War II, of
being a Communist fellow traveler.

Foremost was William F. Buckley, Jr., who, ironically, wrote a
convoluted defense of McCarthy at the time. Buckley's fondness for
two-dollar words was such an affectation that it became difficult at
times to know what he was saying, but he did lend a certain respectability to a conservatism still smarting from disasters stretching all
the way back to the Hoover presidency. In the twilight of his life,
even the reflexive cold warrior Buckley came to regret the invasion
of Iraq as a disaster. Today it would be hard to picture Rush Limbaugh or Sean Hannity playing a Bach partita on the harpsichord as
Buckley did.

Most of the prevailing conservative intelligentsia of the 1960s was associated with Buckley and his *National Review*: William Rusher, who adopted a prosecutorial demeanor reprising E. G. Marshall's roles in *The Caine Mutiny* and *12 Angry Men*; James Burnham, whose single, monomaniacal message was that the Russians were coming; and Russell Kirk, headstone polisher of the memory of Burkean conservatism. As I recall, Kirk would give lectures at Washington foundations while wearing a cape. The last dull reverberation of that movement lingers on in George F. Will, who has had a thirty-year record as a public intellectual unblemished by the expression of a fresh idea.*

Whatever intellectual pretensions these gentlemen sought to inject into the conservative movement and the Republican Party has been overtaken since 1980 by the rise of the religious right. The role of religious fundamentalists in the anti-intellectual and antiscientific stands of the current Republican Party is too obvious to belabor here. Others like Max Blumenthal have commented on it, although it is a topic the major media soft-pedal. But there is another strand in the Republican base that hardly anyone mentions or even notices: the belligerent frat-boy conservative, a political lifestyle and performance art launched in the 1980s by P. J. O'Rourke. It achieved escape velocity the following decade with Rush Limbaugh, Matt Drudge, and the "Brooks Brothers riot" in 2001, when preppy GOP operatives staged fake protests of the Florida recount for the cameras. It culminated in the agent provocateur exploits of the late Andrew Breitbart and his protégé, James O'Keefe.

These men proved that it was possible not to have a single religious bone in your body and still be a Republican in good standing—by sneering at elites and intellectuals. Any nod at Christianity is the

---

* Correction: On March 4, 2012, Will broke his streak by saying that Republicans want to bomb Iran but are afraid of Rush Limbaugh.

tribute vice pays to virtue. Limbaugh got into minor trouble in one such transaction by suggesting that the nominally Christian Lord's Resistance Army of Uganda (LRA) was being persecuted by the crypto-Muslim Barack Obama's pledge of assistance to the Ugandan government in its fight against the LRA. Given that he is a frat-boy Republican who thinks the world terminates twelve miles off the shores of America, Limbaugh did not bother to acquaint himself with the fact that the LRA is a gang of vicious, child-murdering psychopaths. He thought he could get a two-fer by pandering to the religious right with his claim that Christians were being persecuted while feeding raw meat to the rest of his listeners by unveiling yet another one of evil Obama's manifold iniquities.

The Republicans who control the Michigan Senate took a page out of Limbaugh's book in November 2011, when they picked up a Democratic-sponsored bill to prohibit bullying in schools and eviscerated it. Their ploy hinged on creating a "reasons of conscience" loophole—claiming that it was not bullying for one schoolchild to harass another by getting in his face to express a deeply held personal belief—for instance, that the person in question would go to hell because of his assumed sexual orientation. The new bill was passed over the strenuous objections of the opposition, who said that the amendments would in effect license bullying.[2] The fundamentalist base knows how to decode the words—for "conscience" read "religion"—so it was another two-fer: The frat boys could give vent to their sociopathic bullying impulses under a fog of sanctimonious principle. Eventually the bill created so much adverse publicity that Senate Republicans dropped the provision in favor of competing language originating in the Michigan House.

Frat-boy Republicans would contest the notion that the Republican Party wishes to impose a Taliban-style theocracy in America. They display a refreshing lack of moral prudery in their own behavior, which may help explain their sympathy for the conduct of their honorary lodge brother, the street-smart bombthrower Newt Gingrich. Whenever Jesus commands one of them to tread the rocky path to salvation it tends to happen, coincidentally, just prior to a run for public office. But they earn their bona fides by praising belligerence and touting ignorance of world affairs as a moral virtue, notwithstanding the fact that they have no core of fixed moral beliefs at all, religious or intellectual.*

The ultimate apogee of frat-boy conservatism came with the election, in 2000, of a frat-boy president. Some of our reflexive anti-intellectualism can be attributed to the inherent dumbing down that occurs thanks to the natural tendency of our media to focus on human-interest stories in their coverage of political candidates. Partly this is the result of the technical medium involved: The TV camera either loves a person, or it does not. A candidate who is likable, folksy, and has the common touch is far more telegenic than Adlai Stevenson delivering a position paper. And, of course, the media wise guys like to establish narratives that pigeonhole a candidate.

We didn't know much about George W. Bush in 2000, but the press filled in the gap by assuring us that he was the kind of regular guy you could have a beer with. Never mind that he was the fourth generation of an extremely wealthy political dynasty.† Al Gore, by contrast, was a stuffy, pompous bore who claimed to have invented

---

* It is no contradiction to categorize Gingrich, who fancies himself an intellectual, with the anti-intellectuals. His longtime pandering to anti-intellectual themes—i.e., through elite bashing—has been a feature of his rhetorical performance art for decades. Columnist Andrew Sullivan described him during the Republican debates as a "dumb person's idea of a smart person."

† There is also the nonsensical aspect of using the drinking buddy analogy for a recovering alcoholic. That is not a gratuitous disparagement of Bush for having had a problem in his past that he made an effort to resolve. But it was

the Internet. We all had a good laugh at that one. The media framed the narrative to suggest that anyone with intellectual pretensions was an arrogant, out-of-touch elitist with no concern for the common man. And given the fact that the budget was in balance, the nation was at peace, and the press needed a good tabloid human-interest story after the frenzy over Monica Lewinsky had abated, the media delivered prepackaged character sketches of the candidates to us on which to base our voting decisions. Enough voters pulled the lever for Bush, with a little assist from the Supreme Court, to get him over the finish line.

When the 2004 campaign rolled around, the same process repeated itself. George W. Bush, the shoot-first, ask-questions-later cowboy who didn't "do" nuance (meaning intellectual activity), versus John Kerry, the French-speaking windsurfer. That's all we needed to know. Bush, the guy who thought with his gut rather than his cerebrum; and Kerry, the dithering elitist who overanalyzed issues and coiffed his hair. Guess who won.

That is not to say that had Kerry been elected, he would have ushered in a new golden age in the American presidency. I suspect not. But the press might have given the electorate more to go on than the tiresome jock-versus-nerd cliché. They paid less attention to Kerry's 2002 vote to give Bush carte blanche for the invasion of Iraq and what that vote said about his policy judgment. The Authorization of Use of Military Force resolution was a straightforward proposition about whether to invade the wrong country. Since I was a cleared congressional staff member, I read the same thinly sourced, heavily caveated intelligence that Kerry read. It struck me

---

an embarrassing and inappropriate peg on which the media hung a short-hand character study of the man.

then as dubious and tendentious material. He voted for it. The American political system does not suffer from too much thinking and critical analysis; it is becoming crippled by their virtual absence.

☆

An anti-intellectual base requires anti-intellectual leaders, which goes some distance toward explaining the bizarre race for the 2012 GOP presidential nomination. On occasion over the last fifty years a professional comedian such as Pat Paulsen would run for president, and we all appreciated the gag about a joke candidate making absurd statements. But the performance of the more flamboyant Republican candidates in the 2012 contest made it increasingly hard to tell the difference between reality and satire.

For a time, the more nonsensical Herman Cain's statements were, the more popular he became. "Yes, they're a military threat," Cain said about China on the *PBS NewsHour*. "They've indicated that they're trying to develop nuclear capability. . . ."[3] Well, yes, China indicated its intent very forcefully by exploding a nuclear weapon in 1964, which was big news at the time. Cain also said, "When they ask me, 'Who is the president of Ubeki-beki-beki-beki-stan-stan?' I'm going to say, 'You know, I don't know.'" The first and only president of Uzbekistan is Islam Karimov, who tortures and murders his opponents but whose country remains a vital supply route to the Afghanistan war that Cain fervently supports. A piece in *Foreign Policy* about Cain put it this way: "Rather than fake knowledge about this world, he by and large simply expresses contempt for it."[4]

Likewise, we could expect no nuance of any kind from Rick Perry, who explicitly promised as much.[5] He mooted that he might send the U.S. military into Mexico, presumably on the "fight 'em over there so we don't have to fight 'em over here" principle. We know how well that worked out for the last Texan to occupy the Oval Office. Even Mitt Romney, educated at the best schools in the country (though his persona suggests the boss who fired you), has had to hedge his opinion about the evolution of organic life, trying to be all things to all people. He said, "I'm not exactly sure what is meant by intelligent design. But I believe God is intelligent, and I believe he designed the creation. And I believe he used the process of evolution to create the human body."

He topped that performance with his criticism of the Obama administration's foreign policy, which he said seemed to come from the "Harvard faculty lounge" rather than the battlefield. It was an odd criticism for Romney (Harvard MBA, JD) to have made, since his familiarity with Harvard's faculty lounges definitely exceeds his battlefield experience. Thus, even the educated offspring of a cosmopolitan governor has to play the man of the people who sneers at know-it-all elitists from a fancy university—the same university he happens to have attended.

Perhaps the purest expression of the anti-intellectual impulse on the campaign came from veteran culture warrior Rick Santorum. One is tempted to blink in disbelief at the thought that this man spent twelve years in the United States Senate. According to the *Des Moines Register*, here is what transpired at an Iowa university rally: "Discussing controversial classroom subjects such as evolution and global warming, Santorum said he has suggested that 'science should get out of politics.'"[6] Since I was paid to be a budget analyst rather than a theologian, I managed to retire from my career relatively unscathed by any memorable encounter with Santorum during my six years with the Senate.

Whenever the media chance to point out the ignorance (or

feigned ignorance) of a right-wing politician, it will all too often serve as a kind of vindication for the Republican faithful, who will say something along the lines of, The left-wing media (which hardly exists as a major force anymore) is once again trying to smear an honest conservative! He must be doing something right! This is the new Republican victimology: The liberal media is maliciously misrepresenting the views of a rough-hewn but sincere salt-of-the-earth conservative, even when his plain words indict him as an ignoramus or an opportunist.

★

By the turn of the millennium American anti-intellectualism no longer consisted of an unorganized selection of individuals holding quaint or out-of-touch views. It had become a countercultural movement that sought to influence government policy. In line with its institution building in other areas, the right wing created foundations, think tanks, and institutes in order to provide dubious "research" to lend a veneer of respectability and plausibility to its anti-intellectual positions. Many of these think tanks have set their sights on debunking supposedly bogus science.

The Seattle-based Discovery Institute, a nonprofit advocacy organization, has been the most prominent organization spearheading the effort to rebrand creationism as the pseudoscience of "intelligent design." Its principal benefactor for many years has been multimillionaire Howard Ahmanson, Jr., a proponent of theocratic government. The institute's manifesto, the so-called wedge strategy, makes it evident that disinterested scientific research is not on its agenda: It asserts that its mission is to "reverse the stifling dominance of the materialist worldview, and to replace it with a science consonant with Christian and theistic convictions."[7]

Science and religion have for a long time had a bumpy cohabitation. One has only to think of Galileo and the Inquisition, or the nineteenth-century clergy's reaction to Darwin's *Origin of Species*. But up until recently, most Americans appeared to have accepted the basic principles of science taught in high school biology or chemistry class. That is unfortunately no longer the case. The influence of science skeptics is now so pervasive that in 2006 a conservative activist created a knockoff of the online encyclopedia Wikipedia called Conservapedia.[8] Its creator, an offspring of the venerable family values agitator Phyllis Schlafly, believes the earth is six thousand years old, Einstein's theory of relativity is a hoax, and evolutionary biologist Richard Dawkins shares certain characteristics with Adolf Hitler.

The far right's contempt for science and factual evidence dovetails with corporate interests in many areas—climate change; the effect of environmental toxins on health; tobacco;* junk food and obesity; conservation—and how useful that their activities should undermine the scientific evidence behind the drafting of government regulations. When in 2010 the Environmental Protection Agency proposed a rule for establishing greenhouse-gas emission limits for fossil-fuel power plants and petroleum refineries, Republicans were quick to denounce the proposal as scientific quackery. It was obvious, they said, that carbon dioxide was not a pollutant. On the contrary, it was perfectly harmless, because it was present in the very air we breathe. But that argument, while plausible to the casual TV viewer, was carefully intended to distort the real issue. The question was not whether carbon dioxide was breathable but

---

* A fraught if not schizophrenic issue on the religious right: Many fundamentalist churches denounce smoking in harsh moral terms, but millions of their adherents provide the Arbitron ratings for right-wing media personalities such as Limbaugh, who attack attempts to rein in smoking through ordinances and tobacco taxes.

whether adding vast quantities to the atmosphere would have a seriously adverse effect on the climate. If there is a high probability of such an effect, then carbon dioxide could be regulated as an environmental pollutant, regardless of its direct toxicity to humans.

While it is perfectly understandable that coal and oil companies would oppose legislation or regulation limiting greenhouse-gas emissions for purely business reasons, those companies can generally count on sympathetic right-wingers who do not understand the science but who react viscerally to any scientific finding that does not comport with either their gut feelings or the interests of their political contributors. Senator James Inhofe, adducing no empirical evidence, has often stated that the data suggesting humans are responsible for climate change is "a hoax." A fellow Republican in the House, John Shimkus, went further; in March 2009 he opposed the concept of climate change altogether by quoting chapter 8, verse 22, of the Book of Genesis: "[A]s long as the earth endures, seed time and harvest, cold and heat, summer and winter, day and night, will never cease." According to Shimkus, "The earth will end only when God declares its time to be over. Man will not destroy this earth. This earth will not be destroyed by a flood." This is what passes for logic and reason nowadays on Capitol Hill.

☆

George W. Bush was too busy during his monthlong vacation in August 2001 to pay much attention to the August 6 President's Daily Brief that warned of an imminent terrorist attack ("Okay, you covered your ass," he is reported to have told his CIA briefer). What was he doing, aside from playing golf? He was working on his speech about limiting the number of stem-cell lines it was permissible for researchers to use. It was difficult to reconcile sound scientific policy with the demands of his base, but squaring that circle was a more immediate political priority than acting on the warning that Osama bin Laden was determined to strike inside the United States.

By turning science into a malleable tool for ideological exploitation, Republicans are emulating the postmodern critics they profess to despise. For if science is merely a social construct serving the interest of whichever group happens to be ruling society, then the deconstructionists have been vindicated, and the scientific method is no more empirically meaningful than witchcraft or palm reading.

★

Another factor in the rise of anti-intellectualism lies in how the parties have determined which issues are on the table and which are not. Republicans have been more successful in this endeavor than Democrats. For the average American, indeed, for any American, tax policy is hard to understand; the Internal Revenue Code is contained in twenty volumes, and the interactions and unintended effects of changing the law are bewildering. There are hundreds of tax avoidance schemes that individuals and businesses may take advantage of; some are written specifically for a handful of rich persons or for a single firm. The tax write-off for corporate jets is one—how many of us get to ride in a private Gulfstream? Do taxpayers really need to subsidize their travel? Can't these corporate moguls use teleconferencing? Another criticial issue is the Greek debt crisis, which is extremely hard to understand, let alone explain. Or comprehending the national security stakes involved in tracing and decrypting electronic intercepts, or U.S. drone strikes in Pakistan and the accompanying chill they have provoked in our relations with Pakistan's government; these are momentous issues that complicate any assessment of our policy in the region.

Republicans, and many Democrats, do not want a thorough

and accurate national understanding of tax policy, bank regulation, campaign finance, drone policy, or the myriad other complex issues that lie at the heart of governing. It would alienate contributors. So, almost by mutual consent, issues like military interventionism, torture, assassination, U.S. financial support of dictators, and illegal surveillance of the American people are off the table: Too many bureaucrat and contractor toes would get stepped on.

It is a sad commentary on our society that a higher proportion of unlettered sodbusters in the 1880s had an accurate understanding of how banks, railroads, and grain wholesalers worked than the average American today has of how his pension funds are being looted, how he subsidizes corporate jets, or how he—as one individual—should come to pay more federal taxes than the entire General Electric Company. It may be more diverting to watch a televised singing contest than to learn the complex arcana of how American banks leased streetcar lines in Düsseldorf, Germany, to dodge U.S. taxes, but being a fully informed citizen requires sustained intellectual effort.[9]

Owing to the lack of serious and informed popular interest in real issues, we have the current Republican menu of pseudo-issues: abortion, gay marriage, flag burning, prayer in schools, sharia law, and so on. They are simple to grasp and well within the ambit of the average person who does not follow politics. People who wouldn't dream of venturing a thought on the European Financial Stability Fund or the London Interbank Offer Rate have a ready opinion— probably polarized in the usual fashion of American cultural politics—about whether life begins at conception. Of such things are today's American politics made. America's dysfunctional political process forces us all to take a stand on them, and so we have all been dumbed down.

Adding to the public's bamboozlement over the more complex

issues is the cottage industry of publicists, polemicists, and right-wing media personalities that has jumped into the fray. As Jonathan Chait wrote in *The New Republic*:

> Most people are not policy wonks. We rely on trusted specialists to translate these details for us. This is true as well of elected officials and their advisers. Part of the extraordinary vitriol of the health care debate stems from the fact that, on the Republican side, even the specialists believe things that are simply patently untrue. As with climate change and supply-side economics, there isn't even a common reality upon which to base the discussion.

One of the GOP's most common complaints during the health care debate was that Obama's plan would lead to "rationing." This is a scary word that is intended to conjure up visions of queuing up for meager provisions in World War II–era Britain. But if they truly believed in their own free-market dogma, Republicans would have grasped that rationing is inherent in any economic system based on price, exactly as the traditional American health care system has always been. The rich have been able to afford the best health care money can buy, while the poor cannot: That is rationing according to the ability to pay. Republicans ignore this obvious reality in their eagerness to attack Obama's plan to expand health coverage to the previously uninsured.

Paul Krugman opined in one of his columns in the *New York Times*:

> Monetary policy, fiscal policy, you name it, there's a gap. . . . [T]o meet the right's standards of political correctness now, you have to pass into another dimension, a dimension whose

boundaries are that of imagination, untrammeled by things like arithmetic or logic.[10]

Both Chait and Krugman are liberal Democrats, so their statements may sound like partisan polemics. But in explaining the voting preferences of the Republican electorate, veteran GOP pollster Ed Rogers makes the same point: "Even though Cain won't be the nominee, his candidacy tells us a lot about the psychology of GOP activists. Our team wants someone authentic, creative, fresh, bold and likeable. *And we don't have much tolerance for too many facts or too much information.*"[11] (emphasis mine)

★

Rigid ideology and faith-based evidence have created an alternate reality for many Republicans. A Bush administration official, during the period of national chest pounding before the invasion of Iraq, confirmed it. According to journalist Ron Suskind, a senior White House adviser told him the following:

The aide said that guys like me were "in what we call the reality-based community," which he defined as people who "believe that solutions emerge from your judicious study of discernible reality." I nodded and murmured something about enlightenment principles and empiricism. He cut me off. "That's not the way the world really works anymore," he continued. "We're an empire now, and when we act, we create our own reality. And while you're studying that reality—judiciously, as you will—we'll act again, creating other new realities, which you can study too, and that's how things will sort out. We're history's actors . . . and you, all of you, will be left to just study what we do."[12]

People who think like that have already entered the fantasy world of *1984*, where the interrogator O'Brien reveals his philosophy to poor Winston Smith:

> We control matter because we control the mind. Reality is inside the skull. You will learn by degrees, Winston. There is nothing that we could not do. Invisibility, levitation— anything. I could float off this floor like a soap bubble if I wish to. I do not wish to, because the Party does not wish it. You must get rid of these nineteenth-century ideas about the laws of Nature. We make the laws of Nature.

More than just the passage of time separates us from the ideas of progress and education expressed by Eisenhower and his vice president, or Kennedy's New Frontier. There is now a powerful, well-financed countercultural movement that has substantial influence within the GOP. It would roll back the Enlightenment if it could.

10

A LOW DISHONEST DECADE

America's political crisis has been brewing for over thirty years. But in the first decade of the twenty-first century, the sickness threatened to become terminal.

★ ★ ★

Vanity of vanities, saith the Preacher,
vanity of vanities; all *is* vanity.

—Ecclesiastes 1:2.

The first decade of the twenty-first century opened with a farce. The Y2K doomsday scenario, which was supposed to kick in at the stroke of 12:00 A.M., January 1, 2000, turned out to be a joke. Thus began our descent into tragedy. September 11, 2001—a date that everybody knows—and September 15, 2008—when Lehman Brothers filed for bankruptcy—stand in most Americans' minds as bookends for that first decade. The period in between was marked by a strange and paradoxical cultural fusion: The hysterical fear of remorseless terrorism combined with the arrogant vaunting of a country that would redeem the whole world with a sword. These contradictory national impulses were accompanied by a bacchanalia of self-seeking and public looting that made the Teapot Dome scandal seem quaint. This was the decade of Enron, subprime mortgages, Abu Ghraib, color-coded alerts, "heck of a job, Brownie," collateralized debt obligations, the

Troubled Asset Relief Program (TARP)—all culminating in a false promise of hope and change that ran aground in the mud of corporate fund-raising.

The 9/11 attack and the Wall Street collapse resonate in memory because they were the kind of cataclysmic events that occur only a handful of times in a century. But history is not a step function that we can neatly periodize: The past always hangs on into the present, just as the future is always implied by the way we live now. Most Americans did not dance the Charleston and wear raccoon coats all through the 1920s before the crash of '29 landed them in a bread line. That depression was preceded by many signs and portents in the decade before it: a huge and growing income disparity; regressive tax policy; an inflating and collapsing real-estate market; a chronically depressed business sector; and an international banking system that would rapidly transmit the effects of depression in one country around the world. Does any of this sound familiar?

★

The decade of the 2000s began as it ended, with the markets in steep decline after the puncturing of a bubble. The dot-com bubble of the late 1990s was an early sign—one that everyone in power was determined to ignore or conceal, depending on their degree of ignorance—that the growing financialization of the U.S. economy, in tandem with Wall Street's seizure of policy making in Washington, had turned the country's economy into an asset-bubble machine. With the erosion of America's industrial base and the increasing stagnation of the middle class, restless capital could no longer find a lucrative return in investments producing real, tangible wealth that could be sold abroad or consumed at home. So new ways were found to pump up the value of assets—any asset, however shaky on the face of it: Create a buzz about those assets to appeal to the greed and status anxiety of investors, and then dump them before the inevitable collapse. The template was no different from that of the Dutch tulip mania of 1637.

The mounting delusion was fueled by an indulgent government and a credulous prestige press. Pundits had begun to pontificate breathlessly in the mid-1990s about a "new economy" that would overcome the business cycle and create permanent prosperity. The Internet had so revolutionized business models, they opined, that we must be on the cusp of a long period of sustained increase in productivity, low inflation, and low unemployment. Proponents enhanced the allure of their speculations by throwing around jargon like "B2B," "Kondratieff Wave cycle," and "Goldilocks economy." Economics columnists like the *Washington Post*'s James K. Glassman praised the new economy in rhapsodic terms. In 1999 Glassman and Kevin A. Hassett wrote *Dow 36,000: The New Strategy for Profiting from the Coming Rise in the Stock Market*.*

Perhaps the most fateful assistance came from the old maestro himself, Federal Reserve Board chairman Alan Greenspan. By the mid-1990s he, too, was gushing about the new economy when he wasn't too busy lobbying for repeal of the Glass-Steagall Act, which placed a legal firewall between commercial and investment banking. Under Glass-Steagall your savings account could not be put at risk by your bank's speculative ventures. But Greenspan saw Glass-Steagall and other New Deal reforms—indeed, any government regulation—as roadblocks to achieving the self-regulating

---

* Later others would come to appreciate Glassman's promotional talents: In 2007, President Bush nominated him to replace Karen Hughes as undersecretary of state for public diplomacy, and in 2009 he became head of the George W. Bush Institute. Hassett became an economic adviser in 2008 for Republican presidential nominee John McCain.

New Economy. One of my tasks for the House Budget Committee was to pore over Greenspan's soothsayings for statements praising the new economic paradigm. Greenspan was then at the height of his political persuasiveness, and the budget committee's staff director told me that the Fed chairman's statements about the economy could be used to justify a potential deregulatory model in the committee's reports and legislative proposals. The idea was that the report wouldn't simply consist of a bunch of hack congressmen proposing a policy, it would have the implicit endorsement of the all-knowing chairman of the independent Federal Reserve Board. I found no lack of references to suit his needs, although as I parsed through the chairman's various statements, I slowly began to wonder why the ongoing economic boom was fundamentally different from any of the other past booms that had always ended in a bust. In the late 1990s the dot-coms were the darlings of Wall Street, although their business models were absurdly precarious. Who would have thought an online pet food store would become the great hope of venture capitalists? In the period before its initial public offering, the revenues of Pets.com were only about one twentieth of what it spent on advertising, but investors were undeterred. Within a month of its IPO, the bubble burst, and Pets.com shareholders lost $300 million.

Early in 2000, the long slide began. While almost everyone remembers the stock market's panicky drop immediately after 9/11, the Dow actually fell further in the period between Bush's inauguration and 9/11 than it did in the immediate aftermath of the attack. Greenspan's low-interest-rate policy was not an emergency measure passed after the September 2001 attacks but a previously worked out plan to lift the markets after the bubble burst. So were the 2001 Bush tax cuts. During a hearing of the House Budget Committee on March 2, 2001, I listened with a growing sense of unease as Greenspan testified on the state of the economy and the rationale—his rationale, anyway—for the proposed tax cuts. At that time, the Congressional Budget Office was projecting a cumulative ten-year surplus of $5.6 trillion. Greenspan's take:

> These most recent projections, granted their tentativeness, nonetheless make clear that the highly desirable goal of paying off the federal debt is in reach and, indeed, would occur well before the end of the decade.

Pay off the federal debt? Sounds great, doesn't it? Not so, argued Greenspan:

> At zero debt, the continuing unified budget surpluses now projected under current law imply a major accumulation of private assets by the federal government. Such an accumulation would make the federal government a significant factor in our nation's capital markets and would risk significant distortion in the allocation of capital to its most productive uses. Such a distortion could be quite costly, as it is our extraordinarily effective allocation process that has enabled such impressive increases in productivity and standards of living despite a relatively low domestic saving rate.[1]

Translated from the original Greenspan-ese, this means that paying off the debt could be a *bad* thing (notwithstanding his earlier claim that it was a highly desirable goal), because the government would then be in the position of having to meddle in private markets when it invested its surplus. The notion that the United States might, as it approached zero debt, develop a sovereign wealth fund like that of Norway or China was ideological heresy for

Greenspan. From the perspective of 2012, would we rather have our current debt-to-GDP ratio of 100 percent or that of Norway, at *minus* 160 percent? Alan Greenspan thought he knew better, and he provided the keystone in his policy recommendations that helped lay the foundation of our current fiscal crisis. A decade on, instead of sitting on a $5.6 trillion ten-year surplus, as projected in 2001, we found ourselves with a record-breaking ten-year deficit of $6.2 trillion and counting.

To avert the dread consequences of actually being in a position to invest federal assets, Greenspan endorsed the Bush administration's proposed tax cuts. It is probable, in view of his later actions with regard to monetary policy, that he also privately believed the tax cuts would provide investors with extra money to help reverse the falling stock market and reinflate asset prices. Members of Congress may not have understood every word of Greenspan's Delphic mumbo jumbo, but they jumped on the fact that the chairman of the supposedly independent Federal Reserve Board had endorsed the GOP's principal ideological hobbyhorse. After all, it was the people's money. But the people who counted bore a stronger resemblance to the politicians' campaign contributors than to ordinary working stiffs. *Laissez le bon temps rouler!*

☆

Never believe any officeholder, Republican or Democrat, who voted for these tax cuts or for their extension and claims to be concerned about deficits or debts. *The intellectual rationale for the Bush tax cuts as presented by the enormously influential Federal Reserve chairman was precisely to forestall paying off debt.* The whole complex theology about tax cuts paying for themselves or boosting the economy is mainly ex post facto rationalization. The groundwork for the present fiscal crisis was established six months before 9/11, although the ritual squawking, mainly Republican, about debt and deficit was mysteriously shelved until after the 2008 elections. Where were the small-government Republicans during the long eight years of the Bush administration, when their revered leader, with control of both the House and Senate, practically doubled the size of the federal government? I kept waiting for one of them to speak up. But year after year I watched as ever more money was appropriated for the Pentagon, the new and impossibly wasteful Department of Homeland Security, and any number of other schemes cloaked in the ritual justification of national security without the slightest squawk of protest.

But that lay in the future. Throughout the spring and summer of 2001, the Bush administration's national security apparatus kept its eyes firmly averted from the very real possibility of a terrorist striking the United States. The watchword in early 2001 was "Military Transformation." Transformation was a Madison Avenue slogan for paying contractors billions to develop pie-in-the-sky weapon systems of marginal utility that would take two decades to field. It was a relabeling of the so-called revolution in military affairs touted by the Clinton Pentagon only the previous year (the military loves to pour old wine into new bottles). The idea was to keep on building cold war weapon systems but to load them up with even more expensive and hard-to-maintain technology; the justification for these mostly obsolete weapon systems would be backfilled by threat assessments written to order. The notion that roughly two thirds of the thousands of military casualties in the decade ahead would come from primitive homemade bombs concealed in the ground was not on the options menu.

High on the list of potential villains was China, whose forced landing of a U.S. Navy EP-3 reconnaissance aircraft on April Fools' Day 2001 seemed to goad the administration to react in predictable fashion. While circumstances forced it to act in a diplomatically conciliatory way to get the air crew back, it leaked its own newly commissioned defense review that suggested China should now be seen as America's main probable global adversary. At the same time, the Bush administration was already gearing up to attack Iraq, as Treasury Secretary Paul O'Neill, and Richard Clarke, who was the counterterrorism coordinator on the National Security Council, later documented.

When the twin towers fell, the Bush administration's reaction was so chest thumping, scattershot, and authoritarian, its appeal to fear and blind revenge so hyperbolic, that it is not surprising in retrospect that within a year or two millions of people began to believe that 9/11 was a conspiracy orchestrated by the U.S. government.

No, it was not a conspiracy.

Bush and his advisers were unhinged by the failure of their own rigid, ideological, and self-referential thinking to prepare them for the possibility of terrorist attacks. To remedy the situation they fell back on the same patterns of circular logic that caused them to ignore al Qaeda in the first place. This tendency was fatally reinforced by a military-industrial complex that saw (and continues to see) its real mission as achieving the greatest possible throughput of dollars, while it prioritizes threats in proportion to how they might enhance contractors' cash flow. It has become a cliché to suggest that people believe in vast government conspiracies because they cannot believe a handful of private individuals acting on their own, or in loose affiliation, could pull off a hugely consequential event like 9/11. But I think a bigger reason so many people became "9/11 Truthers" is that Bush and his advisers acted in such a high-handed and dictatorial fashion in the weeks, months, and years following the attack. Citizens could be forgiven for imagining that the Bush crowd *must* have been hiding something beneath their strutting and bluster. But the Bush administration behaved exactly as authoritarian governments behave when they are under stress. The events that followed—a needless war, a fractured alliance, the domestic paranoia and infringements of civil liberties—were the fruits of that toxic thinking.

If the actions of the president and his operatives were unworthy of their oaths of office, the behavior of tens of millions of citizens helped enable the pathology of their leaders. There is absolutely no excuse for allegedly free citizens of a democratic country to be so abysmally ignorant of the world around them when they pay taxes (about which they bellyache incessantly) to station hundreds of thousands of U.S. troops in over 150 countries, bribe dictators with billions, and fund uncountable clandestine operations whose potential to backfire is every bit as great as our funding of the Afghan mujahedin in the 1980s. People with enough sophistication to operate an iPhone should be able to locate Yemen or Afghanistan on a world map—and hold their elected officials accountable for what they do in those countries.

I can pinpoint the precise moment when I came to believe Bush and his team had gone off their rockers. The 2002 State of the Union address was the usual staged political circus into which the president's constitutionally mandated message to Congress has in recent decades degenerated. I was watching TV at home with my wife, only half paying attention to the stock political rhetoric, when a curious comment made me sit up and focus intently. After the required emotional blather, Bush got down to business: America was mortally threatened by an axis of evil: Iraq, Iran, and North Korea. Wait a minute! Iran and Iraq were mortal enemies who had fought a decade-long war against each other that left a million casualties. They hated each other like poison! North Korea, the hermit kingdom, might as well have been on the dark side of the moon as far as the other two countries were concerned. You had to have the intellectual honesty and grasp of foreign policy of a political speechwriter to believe those three countries could form an axis of anything.*

Although during the next year the press played the "will he or won't he?" game of speculation as to whether Bush would invade Iraq, from January 2002 onward it seemed obvious to me that he was hell-bent on invading, and was grasping at any pretext to do it. By the time of the perfunctory Authorization of Use of Military Force resolution debate in October 2002, the decision was locked in. Never in U.S. history had a president asked for a declaration of war or its equivalent so long before the commencement of hostilities. It was not only an admission that there was no emergency that would justify a preemptive war, it was also cynically timed less than a month before the congressional midterm elections to apply additional political pressure on a deliberative body that was already borderline hysterical.†

That month I decided that due diligence must be done. After all, it was supposed to be my job, as the lead staffer on defense issues for the House Budget Committee, to poke holes in flawed policy positions. But few members of Congress were systematically questioning the Bush administration's evidence, and the number of skeptical Republicans among them was vanishingly small. To all appearances, their staffs were equally passive and accepting; if any

---

* It turned out that the author of those lines was indeed a White House speechwriter, David Frum, who went on to pen a hagiography of his former boss. It is highly indicative of the downward arc of the decade that in 2010 Frum should have been fired from his position at the American Enterprise Institute because he was insufficiently loyal to right-wing dogma.

† The 2002 midterm election was when Max Cleland was defeated with the help of scurrilous campaign spots suggesting he was aiding and abetting bin Laden.

of them were presenting alternate scenarios to their bosses, I was unaware of it. The Hill, like the rest of the country, was in the grip of a fatalistic march toward war. Being perhaps more optimistic than I am now about the persuasiveness of facts and evidence, I assembled, from unclassified or declassified sources, a one-hundred-page binder of information on Iraq's connection with al Qaeda and its putative possession of weapons of mass destruction. My conclusion was that there was no solid evidence for either assertion. I privately discussed the contents of my findings with a handful of congressmen, as well as my conclusions that the cost of an invasion and occupation of Iraq could greatly exceed the prevailing estimates.* I told those who would listen that I thought the United States might end up creating, in a U.S.-occupied Iraq, a West Bank on steroids. The congressmen did listen politely—one made a mock gesture of burying his head in his hands and said, "I wish you hadn't told me that!" But it did not change their votes. When the vote was held in the House on October 10, 2002, only 6 of 223 Republicans opposed the resolution to go to war. The following day, only 1 of 48 Senate Republicans, Lincoln Chaffee of Rhode Island, voted against it.

Less than a month before the invasion, I was the lead House Budget Committee Republican staffer for the committee's hearing on Iraq. The witness for the Department of Defense was Paul Wolfowitz, the deputy secretary of defense and one of the neoconserva-

---

* The administration's prewar estimates ranged from Deputy Secretary of Defense Paul Wolfowitz's declaration that the invasion might even be free—i.e., paid out of Iraq's oil revenues—to National Economic Council director Lawrence Lindsey's guess that it might cost $100 billion to $200 billion—an indiscretion for which he was fired. The Pentagon's own internal estimate, which it released just prior to the invasion, was $60 billion to $95 billion.

tive architects of the war. Since this was the budget committee, the question on everyone's mind was what the war would cost. While Wolfowitz did his best to dodge giving a firm answer to that question, he attempted to leave the impression that Iraq's oil revenues, plus the release of Iraqi overseas assets that had been frozen by United Nations sanctions, might cover much of the cost. He also did his best to deride the fears of the army chief of staff, General Eric Shinseki, that the occupation of Iraq could require hundreds of thousands of troops. He called such speculations "outlandish" and implied that the military's requirements in Iraq after the war might even be less than in the Balkans during the 1990s. If Congress is often woefully uninformed about national security matters, it is sometimes because the Pentagon willfully misinforms them.

A significant percentage of Americans, from the Beltway elites in their Washington sinecures to Limbaugh's know-nothing dittoheads, believe that the United States can act militarily wherever and whenever it likes with impunity. But the invasion and occupation of Iraq left a trail of evils that will haunt us for decades, not least the cost, which has exacerbated our seemingly intractable fiscal crisis. For along with that other signature Bush policy (the tax cuts), the Bush wars and their associated spending were the largest single policy contributor to the swing from surplus to deficit. I watched this happen from the vantage point of the budget committee and kept waiting for someone to cry foul. Other than one or two gadflies like Ron Paul, the so-called deficit hawks would not question one penny of military spending. At the last count, the Iraq war has cost American taxpayers $824 billion. The Afghan war cost an additional $557 billion. And because these wars were deficit financed, the Treasury had to pay about $300 billion in interest to meet the Pentagon's expenses, making the total cost about $1.7 trillion. If defense were a social program, Republicans would be calling it a manifest failure, and would engage in a vigorous campaign to zero out its budget.

Let us keep in mind that the spending on Iraq and Afghanistan doesn't stop with the Pentagon budget. Congress and the administration added another trillion dollars in associated costs on such things as establishing the Homeland Security Department and increasing the budgets for the State Department and the Veterans Administration. In total, our extravagant and misguided response to 9/11—a tragedy that might have been averted altogether had a few people at the top not diverted their attention to chimerical threats—was responsible directly and indirectly for at least $4 trillion of the $12 trillion slide in the fiscal picture since 2001. Even many liberals don't get this. Paul Krugman has in the past discounted the wars as a significant factor in our vast increase in debt. By refusing to arm themselves with this argument, Democrats and liberal commentators find themselves outgunned, and they get sucked into defending a losing position when the right-wing asserts that entitlements are solely or mainly responsible for deficits. But then, many Democratic politicians already compromised themselves on the war with their votes.

The Iraq disaster revealed something else at once more indefinable and more important than money that helps explain why the last ten years have seemed so grubby and dishonest.

★

It is within the bounds of taste and propriety as defined by the Washington establishment to argue, as I have done, that the invasion and occupation of Iraq was a fiscal extravagance that sorely aggravated the deficit. I could on occasion persuade a Republican officeholder privately to concur with that hypothesis, even if he or

she would not say so publicly. And whether or not the Beltway co-
gnoscenti agree, they will at least entertain as a debatable proposition the argument that the invasion was strategically unwise, and
that it complicated our position in the Middle East. The frenzy of
contractor looting and fraud is certainly on the table for a postmor-
tem, although the establishment's zeal to punish the perpetrators
has been lukewarm at best. One can even make the argument that
Iraq was a public relations disaster that blackened the image of the
United States abroad. You could argue any of those propositions on
a Sunday morning talk show or publish them in an op-ed in the
mainstream media—the *New York Times*, say—and no one would
think too much of it.

What you must never, ever, say, however, is that the invasion of
Iraq was morally indefensible and a premeditated crime for which
the people responsible should be held legally accountable. To do so
would result in the same averted eyes and embarrassed cough behind the hand, as if you had eaten the hostess's mashed potatoes
with a soup spoon at a Georgetown dinner party. It would be more
likely that you'd not be invited back to the talk show circuit than the
dinner table faux pas would get you stricken from a future guest
list.

I am not much of a believer in the idea that a broad sample of
humanity is likely to vary significantly from another broad sample
of humanity in terms of personal moral rectitude. In our private
behavior we are probably no better or worse than our ancestors
were, and Americans are unlikely to be innately much better or
worse than Swedes, say, or Italians. But under the pressure of
group norms we can be influenced to behave, particularly when
acting under the shield of official duties, in ways we would never
contemplate acting in our private capacity. The famous (or infa-
mous) Milgram Experiment and dozens of other psychological

tests since then have confirmed that the pressure to conform to an authority figure or peer group can cause people to behave in shocking ways.[2]

Based on my own experience in government, I am not surprised that functionaries caught up in "the mission," and acting within a conformist and hierarchical bureaucratic culture, could behave in ways immoral and contrary to domestic statutes and international treaties. Naturally, such persons would loudly proclaim their innocence and protest that they had acted in good faith, guided by the noble motive of patriotism or the best information available at the time. What is more interesting, in a morbid way, is how people with no direct culpability in those crimes have thrown a screen of protection around the perpetrators. Others in government, the media, and so-called opinion leaders generally have been conspicuously silent about these crimes.

Only low-ranking enlisted personnel were punished for the torture at Abu Ghraib: "Different spanks for different ranks," as the military saying goes.* But what are we to think about the people higher up the food chain who sanctioned or encouraged the torture? Or those who unleashed the war in the first place? Despite the elaborate efforts of the Bush administration to disguise the Iraq war as an exercise in self-defense, it was clearly a war of aggression, a crime described by Justice Robert Jackson, the lead U.S. prosecutor at the Nuremberg war crimes tribunals after World War II, as follows:

---

* As retired Army colonel and author Andrew Bacevich has noted, the one high-ranking officer who was reprimanded and reduced in rank because of Abu Ghraib was the exception that proved the rule. Brigadier General Janis L. Karpinski, the commandant of the prison, was a female and a reserve officer to boot—not part of the favored West Point crowd. And her dereliction of duty charge had no connection with any abuses, according to the Pentagon inspector general.

To initiate a war of aggression, therefore, is not only an international crime; it is *the supreme international crime*, differing only from other war crimes in that it contains within itself the accumulated evil of the whole.[3]

What about people like John Yoo, the deputy assistant attorney general in the Justice Department and author of the "torture memo," who defined presidential power in such a way that all constitutional protections, law, treaties, and morality itself could be set aside at will? Yoo said the following in a 2004 debate with Douglas Cassel, a Notre Dame legal scholar:

Cassel: If the president deems that he's got to torture somebody, including by crushing the testicles of the person's child, there is no law that can stop him?

Yoo: No treaty.

Cassel: Also no law by Congress—that is what you wrote in the August 2002 memo. . . .

Yoo: I think it depends on why the president thinks he needs to do that.

Is Yoo languishing in some federal prison for violating our statutes regarding torture, which is a crime? No, he is currently a professor of law at the University of California, Berkeley, visiting professor at the University of Chicago, and a visiting scholar at the American Enterprise Institute. President Obama and Attorney General Holder prefer to look forward, not backward. An ethical chasm separates the Great and the Good of contemporary Washington from the principle that Justice Jackson expressed at Nuremberg:

> Any resort to war is a resort to means that are inherently criminal. War inevitably is a course of killings, assaults, deprivations of liberty, and destruction of property. An honestly defensive war is, of course, legal and saves those lawfully conducting it from criminality. But inherently criminal acts cannot be defended by showing that those who committed them were engaged in a war, when war itself is illegal. The very minimum legal consequence of the treaties making aggressive wars illegal is to strip those who incite or wage them of every defense the law ever gave, and to leave warmakers subject to judgment by the usually accepted principles of the law.[4]

And here is Jackson's reproof against the notion of American Exceptionalism, the idea that "if America does it, it's OK."

> If certain acts of violation of treaties are crimes, they are crimes whether the United States does them or whether Germany does them, and we are not prepared to lay down a rule of criminal conduct against others which we would not be willing to have invoked against us.[5]

The decision to initiate an unprovoked war of aggression was, as Justice Jackson stressed, inseparable from the crimes that followed. It would hardly do to limit the focus of our attention to a miserable creature like Yoo, because all who voted for the Authorization of Use of Military Force resolution bear at least some responsibility for the atrocities that followed. Whether they let war hysteria override their collective judgment, or were too intellectually lazy to check the evidence, or cravenly feared that a no vote would be politically harmful, these officials failed in their duty to the country and to those who sent them to Washington.

But it is not enough to say that Abu Ghraib, or the renditions of prisoners to countries (including Syria) that enthusiastically tortured them, or the contractor corruption, or the decline in American prestige abroad both among foreign governments and their publics, or the fiscal damage caused by the war were all predictable consequences of the decision to go to war in the first place. I believe the toxic dynamic that led to all of these ills is one, the same, and inseparable from the belligerent and avaricious mind-set that deregulated the markets, pushed the tax cuts, encouraged subprime borrowing, and botched the handling of Hurricane Katrina. The bedrock of this mind-set is a lack of intellectual seriousness combined with ideological rigidity, sound-bite glibness, and ethical corner cutting. And power worship, whether the object of worship is money, high office, or military might. The cultural witch's brew of the last thirty years produced Ken Lay and Bernie Madoff just as surely as it produced John Yoo and Dick Cheney.

In 2006, former Watergate figure John Dean wrote a book called *Conservatives Without Conscience*. It drew heavily on Robert Altemeyer's psychological studies.* Dean wrote at length about such well-known political figures as Gingrich and DeLay, describing their ruthlessness, ethical corner cutting, and superhuman ability to constantly change their stories and keep a straight face. He

---

* Also in 2006, Altemeyer wrote a more popularly accessible condensation of his and other researchers' clinical studies titled *The Authoritarians* (http://members.shaw.ca/jeanaltemeyer/drbob/TheAuthoritarians.pdf).

also profiled Bush administration figures such as Cheney, Yoo, David Addington,* and Bush himself. His conclusion: These people's obsessive drive for personal power, their ruthlessness in exercising it, their recklessness and heedlessness of the consequences, and their blind faith in their own righteousness makes them authoritarian personalities, to be sure, but also exactly the wrong people to be holding power in a representative government.

This type of persona is hardly exclusive to the world of politics. In 2011 the German magazine *Der Spiegel* published a report on research at the University of St. Gallen in Switzerland that found traders at financial firms took risks greater even than those a clinical psychopath would take.[6] And this was not only to get rich on their own accounts: "It was most important to the traders to get more than their opponents," an official familiar with the research said. "And they spent a lot of energy trying to damage their opponents." That would seem to corroborate what I have seen over the many years I had a chance to observe this personality type strutting the halls of Congress. Whatever his—for this type is mostly, although not exclusively, male—announced policy goal may be, that objective is both mutable and unimportant in the larger scheme of things. What is crucial is that his own power be vindicated, and his real or perceived enemies crushed. Newt Gingrich is a museum-piece example of this type of authoritarian personality: He has vacillated between the view that health care mandates are a panacea and the work of the devil; he engineered the impeach-

---

* David Addington was an adviser to Cheney and the principal advocate of the theory of the "unitary executive." Stripping away the legalistic weasel words, the theory held that anything the president does is by definition legal. It is the equivalent of Richard Nixon's view of executive power as expressed to David Frost: "Well, when the president does it, that means that it is not illegal."

ment of President Clinton while entangled in his own extramarital affair; in 1995, during his epic struggle against Clinton over the government shutdown, he praised the Congressional Budget Office as an impeccably neutral arbiter of budgetary legislation, only to denounce it in late 2011 as a reactionary socialist cabal that he would abolish. The positions change, but the vitriolic denunciations and relentless desire for personal power remain. In 1978, at the beginning of his career, Gingrich told a group of College Republicans: "[O]ne of the great problems we have in the Republican Party is that we don't encourage you to be nasty." An alleged political virtue of Democrats at the time, according to Gingrich, was that the party produced "nasty people who had no respect for their elders."[7]

The first decade of the twenty-first century was a period stamped with the imprint of this type of authoritarian personality, whether in government or on Wall Street. And there were tens of millions of Americans who, although lacking the personal gumption, ambition, and leadership qualities of a Gingrich or a DeLay, nevertheless empowered them to achieve their goals. Altemeyer describes these types as "authoritarian followers." They are socially rigid, highly conventional, and strongly intolerant personalities who, absent any self-directed goals, seek achievement and satisfaction by losing themselves in a movement greater than themselves. One finds them overrepresented in reactionary political movements, fundamentalist sects, and leader cults like Scientology. They are the folks tailor-made to respond as intended when told, for example, as Bush's press secretary Ari Fleischer said after 9/11, that they had better "watch what they say"; or who nod approvingly at illegal surveillance because, if you have nothing to hide, you have nothing to fear; or who, after months of news stories saying that no weapons of mass destruction had been found in

Iraq, nevertheless insist on believing that they *were* found. Alte-meyer:

> Probably about 20 to 25 percent of the adult American pop-ulation is so right-wing authoritarian, so scared, so self-righteous, so ill-informed, and so dogmatic that nothing you can say or do will change their minds. They would march America into a dictatorship and probably feel that things had improved as a result.... And they are so submissive to their leaders that they will believe and do virtually anything they are told. They are not going to let up and they are not going away.

Twenty to 25 percent is not a majority, but it is enough to swing an election, especially when you consider that the authoritarian fol-lower is more easily organized and mobilized than the rest of the population. Altemeyer closed with the admonition that such per-sonality types "are not going away." The rise of the Tea Party after 2008 showed that he was a far better prognosticator than Sidney Blumenthal, who thought that the radical takeover of the GOP had "shattered the party."

Democrats appear to be somewhat less subject to this authori-tarian leader-follower syndrome. As Will Rogers remarked, "I don't belong to any organized party; I'm a Democrat." By contrast, if there is anything the GOP has mastered, it is falling into line be-hind the dogma of the moment.* That said, the pathology is not

---

* Between 1994 and 2008, an individual health-care mandate was a standard GOP nostrum, promoted not only by Mitt Romney, but by Newt Gingrich when he was the highest elected Republican official in the country, and it was endorsed by the conservative Heritage Foundation. Now the mandate is the work of the devil, and authoritarian followers of the GOP, like faithful

unknown in the party of Jefferson: Scratch a Rahm Emanuel or a John Edwards and one finds the same sort of imperious authoritarian one sees on the other side of the ideological divide. And former New Jersey senator and governor Jon Corzine offers up the same sort of hypocritical moralizing and ethical corner cutting that we find in Republicans like Gingrich. Although to a lesser extent than Republicans on Iraq, Democrats have shown a disturbing tendency to buy into the Obama administration's questionable premises on Afghanistan, Pakistan, and the escalating drone campaign.

The tribal behaviors of the leaders and followers of both parties have been similar enough that remarkably little has changed since the supposedly epochal election of 2008. For all the talk of hope and change, our national security landscape is substantially the same. It is less ostentatiously theatrical than it was under the Bush administration, but it is roughly equivalent in substance, if not style.

And what about the handling of the financial crisis? Has Tim Geithner acted differently in any significant way than Hank Paulson would have? Have any of the top tier of Wall Street malefactors done jail time? On the contrary, efforts at legal redress have been so skimpy that some courts have been rejecting the Securities and Exchange Commission's proposed settlements with the big banks on the grounds that they are derisory in view of the damage the banks have done. The Obama administration has to a great extent punted the country's economic policy, for good or ill, to the unelected Federal Reserve Board.

In 2003, when the Bush administration engineered the Medi-

---

party members in Orwell's *1984*, believe "we've always been at war" against mandates.

care Prescription Drug Act, it was overtly planned as a payday for Big Pharma. The statute was rigged to prohibit the negotiation of drug prices and to prevent the reimportation of prescription medicines from Canada. Like magic, the money rained down on the vultures of K Street, including Gingrich and his corporate-funded Center for Health Transformation. In 2009, when Obama proposed the Affordable Care Act, one of the first things he did was obtain a buy-in from Big Pharma that effectively protected its profitable market rigging. Similar deals protected the insurers. Was it because he knew these interests were too strong to fight? Was it because he was conflict averse by nature and too readily sought a bad compromise? Or was it a calculation that the Democratic Party would need the contributions when the next election cycle came around? It makes no difference; the practical effect is exactly the same.

The great irony, camouflaged by the Republicans' moronic "Obama, the Kenyan socialist" rhetoric and the uproar over the Tea Party, is that the major thrust of policy in the United States remained much the same after 2008 as it was before. The outward form of Bush corporate Republicanism had pretty much played itself out politically, and everybody, even the GOP, was tired of it. Obama and the Democrats essentially stepped into the shoes of the Republicans and followed the same basic policy line, rebranded under the rubric of hope and change. There were of course modifications of emphasis, and some of the more egregious aspects of the previous administration were downplayed, but there was far more continuity than change.

And rather than engage in soul-searching about the more destructive policies of the Bush administration—the war in Iraq, the tax cuts, the negative results of outsourcing and so-called free trade—the GOP leadership decided the only necessary policy was

188 ☆ THE PARTY IS OVER

to be the *anti-Obama party*. With that as the sole plank in their platform—the rest could be filled in later—Republicans rushed out to Astroturf the ostensibly independent Tea Party, which, as we have seen, was in reality the activist core of the Republican base. It was easy enough to take all the inchoate venom that had built up over the previous decade thanks to 9/11, the culture wars, and the economic collapse of 2008 and focus it against Obama. Anti-Obamaism became the signature Republican political philosophy of the second decade of the century. The Tea Party's supposedly spontaneous origin in 2009 was in reality anything but accidental. The previous twenty years of well-funded networking, assisted by propaganda bullhorns like Rush Limbaugh, Fox News, and all the rest, had laid the groundwork for the emergence of an angry and rigidly inflexible new movement.

The crowning irony is that the preposterous attacks against Obama actually did the president a favor by masking his true political makeup: that of a corporate centrist who basically followed (with minor variations) the main policy line of his predecessor. After the greatest economic collapse in eighty years, a collapse predominately (although not exclusively) caused by the irresponsibility of corporate finance, the net result was a parallel shift by both established parties *to the right*: the Democrats to a vaguely center-right corporate-friendly status quo party that preserves vestiges of the social safety net for appearance's sake, and the Republicans to a fend-for-yourself leader-follower cult of conspiracies and Armageddons, of endless enemies and religious crusades.

As W. H. Auden said of an earlier period of world crisis, all the clever hopes expire of a low dishonest decade.

11

ARE THE DEMOCRATS
ANY BETTER?

**As Republicans have grown ideologically more
rigid, Democrats have almost entirely ceased to have
any core beliefs at all—and their grab for corporate
money is as egregious as that of the GOP.**

★ ★ ☆

They've got a set of Republican waiters on one side and
a set of Democratic waiters on the other side, but no matter
which set of waiters brings you the dish, the legislative grub
is all prepared in the same Wall Street kitchen.

—Huey Pierce Long, in a speech for the reelection
of Senator Hattie Caraway (D-Arkansas), 1932

If you seek a poster child for the corporatization of the Democratic Party, you need look no farther than Jon Corzine, the now disgraced former senator and governor from New Jersey. Like Chuck Schumer, Max Baucus, and Chris Dodd, Corzine is the very model of a Wall Street Democrat. In 2000, when he decided the time had come to step down from his position as the CEO of Goldman Sachs, he bought a seat in the Senate representing New Jersey with $62 million of the compensation he had extracted from Goldman. (This hardly made a dent in his personal wealth, for he had made $400 million when the company went public.[1]) Both parties love self-financing candidates, as it means they can concentrate their vast but finite party war chests on other races. In 2005, after less than a full term in the Senate, Corzine went on to run for governor of New Jersey; when his personal expenditure for that race is added to the amount he spent for his Senate seat, the combined total comes to over $100 million.*

When the New Jersey citizenry bounced him from office in November 2009, Corzine landed on his feet as CEO and chairman of MF Global, an offshoot of a British investment company dating to 1783. He deployed his considerable business acumen to tank MF Global within eighteen months. His major project was to generate increased financial returns for the firm (and himself) by investing $6 billion in the debt instruments of Portugal, Italy, Ireland, and Spain at the precise point when Europe was sliding into financial crisis. It was a business strategy about as shrewd as buying Confederate bonds after the fall of Atlanta, and Corzine forced out a company executive who objected. When the company collapsed and Congress inquired about the $1.2 billion of clients' money that had been commingled with the bad investment, Corzine was profusely apologetic. But when asked whether he would make restitution to investors out of his own wealth, he said no.

One wonders why the Democrats, the supposed party of the common folk, were so accommodating to an amoral predator like Jon Corzine. Was he an anomaly, a bad apple? Only if Robert Rubin or Timothy Geithner could also be considered anomalies: The first helped engineer the deregulation of financial markets to his own

---

* Excluding the gold-plated Senate campaigns of Corzine and Hillary Clinton, in 2000 the average cost of a Senate seat was $4.7 million. Corzine spent $38 million in the 2005 governor's race; his opponent, Doug Forrester, $19 million.

benefit and that of his former colleagues at Goldman Sachs;* the second was asleep at the switch at the New York Federal Reserve Bank during the prelude to the Wall Street meltdown. (After becoming Treasury secretary, Geithner successfully lobbied Congress not to pass legislation that would prevent AIG from paying out $218 million in bonuses to employees after the insurance giant had received $170 billion in bailout funds from the taxpayers.) The two men are not so different from Republican counterparts like former senator Phil Gramm of Texas, who assisted Rubin in deregulating Wall Street before jumping to a lucrative sinecure as vice chairman of the Swiss bank UBS, or Rick Scott, the current governor of Florida, who was implicated in 1997 in the largest Medicare fraud case in history; he resigned as CEO of Columbia/HCA after the company was fined $1.7 billion and found guilty of defrauding the government.[2]

As I watched the health-care debacle unfold in the Senate in 2009, the nexus between big corporate money and Democratic behavior became manifest. For reasons that may become clear only when we read Obama's White House memoir, the president punted operational control of the legislation to Congress. That meant it ended up in the lap of Democrat Max Baucus of Montana, the chairman of the Senate Finance Committee. His fund-raising prowess is legendary: Baucus received $4 million between 2003 and 2008 from the health-care industry that his committee has jurisdiction over. As soon as the committee's deliberations began, Baucus declared a single-payer solution "off the table." Whether or not single-payer had a realistic chance of becoming law, by exclud-

---

* President Clinton called Rubin, who made $126 million in cash and stock options at Citigroup, "the greatest Treasury Secretary since Alexander Hamilton."

ing it as leverage at the outset, Baucus unilaterally disarmed any possibility of extracting concessions from the health-care industry. The resulting bill mollified all the major health-care interests, including the insurance industry and Big Pharma. While the Patient Protection and Affordable Care Act may have accomplished some praiseworthy goals, such as expanding coverage to more Americans, it flunked miserably on correcting the principal flaw in U.S. health care: Our system is 50 percent more expensive than that of the thirty-four countries of the OECD while providing no better patient outcomes. And by providing for an individual mandate requiring citizens to purchase privately supplied health insurance, Baucus, with Obama's acquiescence, placed the law in constitutional jeopardy

Baucus is also noteworthy in that an extraordinary number of his former staffers—about two dozen—have gone on to become K Street lobbyists. In the case of the health-care debate, one of them, a health-care lobbyist, parachuted back into a finance committee position to help write the Affordable Care Act. If the current revolving door between K Street and the Hill sounds similar to that of the relationship between Tom DeLay and superlobbyist Jack Abramoff, the similarities don't end there: In the early 2000s, Baucus received at least nineteen thousand dollars in contributions from Abramoff, and also availed himself of Abramoff's skybox at the Verizon Center in Washington.

But isn't there a pragmatic "lesser of two evils" argument to be made for the Democrats? For sure, they are tainted by money, but aren't they simply playing by the rules of the game that is rigged by money? Aren't they generally better than the Republicans, who are Neanderthals on social issues and seemingly crazy for war? Unfortunately, while there is much to be said for pragmatism, our campaign finance and conflict of interest laws did not fall out of the heavens; Democrats were heavily involved in shaping them.*

As for their greater trustworthiness on national security, that is not self-evident, however much Democrats may think they are saner and sounder than Republicans on issues of war and peace. In 2008, rank-and-file Democrats who had opposed the Bush administration's constant warmongering saw what they wished to see in candidate Obama. He campaigned against the Iraq war but pointedly said Afghanistan was the "good war." Nevertheless, those who voted for him assumed that his opposition to Iraq meant that he would be disposed to end, as rapidly as was feasible, even a war he supported.

Those hopes turned out to be illusory. If he was going to oppose one war, he wanted to protect himself by supporting another, more popular war. Perhaps he wanted to inoculate himself against the perennial Republican campaign charges that any Democratic candidate for the presidency is "weak on national security," or an appeaser. While many pundits have asserted that Obama was not being dishonest in his campaign speeches, as he only criticized the invasion and occupation of Iraq and not of Afghanistan, his subsequent actions were deceptive even with respect to Iraq. Obama's planned date to withdraw from Iraq was the same as that of the outgoing Bush administration: December 31, 2011. Given that this date was three years into Obama's term in office, it would hardly have been a precipitous withdrawal. Yet throughout the entire time leading up to the deadline, the Obama administration attempted to undo the timetable and conditions of the withdrawal

* Democrats are on somewhat firmer ground with the *Citizens United* case, as the Supreme Court appointees of Democratic presidents dissented from that decision.

plan. The December 4, 2008, Status of Forces Agreement that the Bush administration achieved with the Maliki government in Baghdad provided that, along with the withdrawal of U.S. military forces by the end of 2011, the legal immunity from Iraqi prosecution that U.S. troops had enjoyed would end. That may have been the key feature of the whole agreement: After years of suffering civilian deaths, the Iraqis were in no mood to continue to provide immunity to U.S. combat forces. But there was no way the Pentagon was going to operate in Iraq without that immunity. Throughout the Obama presidency, Defense secretaries Robert Gates and Leon Panetta shuttled back and forth between Washington and Baghdad pleading with the Maliki government to give U.S. forces the immunity they would need to stay past the deadline.

It might seem strange that the president would allow a subordinate, a cabinet secretary, particularly a Republican like Gates, to undermine an achievement that he could point to as a sign that he had kept his political promise to the millions of Americans who had elected him. Three theories could explain this. One explanation is that President-elect Obama, as an inexperienced new chief executive eager to appear a centrist, allowed Gates to dictate the terms under which he would serve in a Democratic administration.* According to that theory, Obama abdicated national security policy to an unelected permanent government of defense technocrats. Another explanation is that underneath his hope-and-change rhetoric Obama was a centrist, if not a center-rightist, in his true foreign policy inclinations; he let subordinates do the dirty work while he remained above the fray and collected his Nobel Peace

---

* I have one defense industry source (albeit only one) who says that this is what happened. If true, it could explain why DOD budget requests under Obama were *higher* than those projected by the outgoing Bush administration for the period after 2009.

Prize. A third possibility is that his fear of appearing weak on defense was such that he would make no move on foreign policy that would give an opening for Republican attacks. In any case, all these theories lead to the same result: The Obama administration's national security policies are, nuances aside, substantially the same as those of the Bush administration.

In the end, the Maliki government held firm to its demand, and Obama made a virtue of necessity, trumpeting the troop withdrawal as a promise kept. But two further developments with regard to Iraq make one doubtful both as to the president and his loyal Democratic followers in Congress. On November 29, 2011, Senator Rand Paul offered an amendment to the defense authorization bill that would declare the 2002 Authorization of Use of Military Force resolution in Iraq to have expired. Notwithstanding Senator Paul's reputation as a right-winger, like his father he bucks the trend in the GOP when it comes to military intervention. As might be expected, he only garnered three other GOP votes for his amendment. But what about the Democrats? They nominally controlled the chamber and had made such a fuss about Bush's Iraq policy in the 2006 election campaign. Only twenty-five of the fifty-three senators who caucus with the Democrats voted for Rand Paul's amendment. Whether the opponents voted from conviction or as obedient water carriers for an administration that opposed the amendment is irrelevant. The Democratic chairman of the Armed Services Committee, Carl Levin, who was among the high-profile opponents, resorted to the tiresome cliché that it would tie U.S. commanders' hands. How, exactly, if the troops they commanded had already been withdrawn and America was out of the war?

The other sign that even now we haven't quite reached "mission accomplished" in Iraq is implicit in the administration's plan for its civilian presence in that country. The total number of State Department and other foreign affairs agencies' employees, plus support and security contractors, is expected to reach approximately seventeen thousand during the year after the troop withdrawal. That is roughly the size of an army division. State will, incidentally, be buying up to 110 Sikorsky S-61 helicopters over the next five years, supposedly for its day-to-day role worldwide (which hitherto was satisfied by renting or leasing helicopters as needed, suggesting that a disproportionate share of these new helicopters will find service in Iraq). Quite apart from the expense, the 110 S-61s would give State almost as big a fleet as the 137 helicopters operated by the U.S. Coast Guard, which patrols a coastline over twelve thousand miles long, in addition to the Great Lakes and inland waterways. The Obama administration's solution to a hypertrophied and disproportionately influential Pentagon is not to cut back on the DOD but to militarize other agencies.

One can barely catalogue the Democrats' many objections, over the course of George W. Bush's presidency, to his extraordinary grab for unconstitutional executive powers and his law breaking (think of illegal surveillance, torture, and the detention of prisoners without charge). But when January 20, 2009, dawned, all those objections miraculously disappeared. If Bush's policies were a dangerous excursion from constitutional practices, what are we to say now that Barack Obama has consolidated, institutionalized, and expanded those practices? Even Bush did not claim the unilateral executive right to kill U.S. citizens based on evidence only he could see, as Obama has done with his greatly expanded campaign of targeted assassinations using unmanned aerial vehicles in Pakistan, a state with 180 million people, one hundred nuclear weapons, and the potential to make our debacle in Iraq look like a sideshow. (President Ford issued an executive order explicitly banning assassinations after the CIA excesses of the 1970s, but no one seems terribly concerned about that now.)[3] The majority of rank-and-file Democrats are quiescent, particularly members of Congress. In their eagerness to rubber-stamp these power grabs, the Democrats who control the Senate passed legislation to extend and expand presidential powers granted by the 2001 Authorization of Use of Military Force resolution. In addition, the majority of Senate Democrats ratified the Bush administration's claim that it should have the power to arrest U.S. citizens on U.S. soil and detain them indefinitely without charge. That outrageous breach of due process is now the law of the land.

On March 5, 2012, Attorney General Eric Holder finally provided a public justification for the administration's unprecedented claim that it could kill U.S. citizens at will. His perfunctory rationale amounted to saying that the persons so targeted were not denied due process, because the Constitution's guarantee of due process does not necessarily grant judicial process. In short, we don't need a judge to declare you guilty and execute you. This legal theory might have surprised the Framers of the Constitution.

Many left-leaning think tanks, like the Center for American Progress, handle the same executive branch usurpations that they criticized when Bush was in office less by explicitly praising them (for that would be too blatantly hypocritical) as by adopting a see-no-evil approach. A pervasive mentality appears to have taken over among establishment Democrats that we live under a government of men (and women) rather than laws. Illegal surveillance, indefinite detention, unlimited executive war powers, and the whole menu of executive branch encroachments were a grave breach of the Constitution, decency, and common sense when practiced by a Republican president. But now that a Democrat is in office, it is different. He is one of our people and can be trusted to wield power responsibly. He won't spy on us. He won't detain us without charge.

There's no way he will assassinate us (a power Bush never explicitly claimed). With this attitude, establishment Democrats only mirror the right-wing Republicans who cheered the PATRIOT Act, denounced criticism of illegal wiretapping, and favored all manner of illegality. They believed that they, too, were immune from having their rights violated by the government so long as "their guy" was in power.

Given that Democratic administrations are more inclined than Republican ones to espouse domestic reform policies that cost a lot of public money, it is telling that Obama has squandered hundreds of billions of dollars on Afghanistan during his first term, while having to fight protracted battles with Republicans merely to get unemployment insurance extended. Likewise, his modest public infrastructure plan (which has gone nowhere) is "paid for" by offsetting revenue increases, while he never attempted to pay for the war (which entails vastly larger sums), either with tax increases or spending cuts elsewhere in the budget. Obama has increased our expenditures in Afghanistan from $59.5 billion in the last year of the Bush administration to $115.1 billion for 2012. By the end of his first term in office his administration will have spent $413 billion on Afghanistan. Perhaps it has never occurred to Obama or his advisers that domestic reform agendas can run aground because of divisive and expensive foreign wars, as Lyndon Johnson discovered to his peril.

The DOD budget grew more under Obama than it had been projected to grow by the Bush administration. Various illegal or unconstitutional regimes involving surveillance, detention, and trial instituted by Bush have been retained, consolidated, and strengthened under Obama. On the domestic front, Timothy Geithner, Obama's Wall Street messenger boy, saw to it that there would be no

CEO compensation limits in the Dodd-Frank bill, and that the bill as a whole would be more façade than substance.

Now that Obama has stabilized the plutocracy he promised to reform, the owners of this country may look upon him as potentially dispensable as a two-term presidential aspirant. In a deep and intractable recession one can never discount the possibility that a Republican could win the presidency against an incumbent Democrat. But if the GOP nominates a candidate too deeply flawed or too right wing to be plausible, it won't really matter. The main thrust of the establishment's policies will be implemented regardless of who wins. That is the genius of our two-party system.

Birth certificates, death panels, sharia law, and all the other so-called issues that have roiled us for the past few years are the kabuki theater of American politics, like the May Day parades in the old Soviet Union. Far away from the political stage of make-believe, and behind the closed doors of corporate America, is where the real show goes on, and where the real decisions are made.

12
A WAY OUT?

What changes are necessary to right the ship of state?

★ ★ ★

We have now sunk to a depth at which re-statement
of the obvious is the first duty of intelligent men.

—George Orwell, review of *Power: A New Social Analysis*
by Bertrand Russell in the magazine *Adelphi*, January 1939

As we embark on the second decade of the twenty-first century, the commanding heights of corporate America—the banks, the military-industrial complex, corporate interests benefiting from huge subsidies like Big Pharma and Big Oil—largely have the government they want. They have the tax structure they desire. Under Bush appointee Chris Cox, the SEC's regulatory function was wrecked. The military has been so outsourced that the Army can no longer feed itself, while a policy of permanent war assures a perpetual cash flow to contractors. Federal law guarantees pharmaceutical companies the kind of collusive and monopolistic profiteering that antitrust laws were intended to prevent. Corporate America has posted record profits even amid the most protracted period of joblessness in post–World War II history. It is corporate nirvana.

Under these circumstances, who needs an activist government?*

---

* Apart from the Medicare Prescription Drug Act and the lucrative war and
homeland security cash flows, the Bush administration engineered the No

Now that the commanding heights have achieved their objectives, a gridlocked government will work just fine, regardless of who is in charge. In any case, both parties are so dependent on corporate money for their existence that it is hard to tell them apart. When the usual cultural wars distraction ran its course—in 2011 the new Republican House initially concentrated on abortion rather than the economy—the next order of business was strident calls for immediate spending cuts in the middle of the worst recession since World War II—an action that most economists believe would contract the economy further. What they would not do is rein in the banks that were largely responsible for the recession in the first place, as a necessary precondition for a program of economic reconstruction that would also include long-term and sustainable deficit reduction.

The calculation from the top may be that the public has already forgotten how the trillion-dollar annual deficits were created in the first place: by the Bush fiscal policies, of course, but also by the transfer of trillions of dollars in illiquid (and largely useless) bank assets onto the public balance sheet thanks to the Treasury Department and the Federal Reserve. The scam was this: The banks unloaded their debts onto the taxpayer, and then the fiscal hawks dutifully began screaming about how we were drowning in debt and how Social Security and Medicare were responsible. Cuts in your earned benefits will pay for the banks' bad loans. Beautiful!

Congress played along with the game. The banksters could count on gonzo Republicans to thwart even the baby steps that some Democrats took to confront the economic crisis—when the large number of business Democrats in the Senate or the Obama

---

Child Left Behind Act, largely as a sop to the school privatization industry and the educational testing racket, and the 2005 bankruptcy revisions making it harder for consumers to discharge debt.

administration itself did not beat them to the punch. Congress sank so low in public esteem that it barely ranked above Fidel Castro in popularity. The Senate has come to resemble Kevin Phillips's description of that chamber in an earlier time:

> The U.S. Senate through the convulsive 1890s remained a citadel of millionaire industrialists, an aptly arrogant metaphor for the late Gilded Age. The Senators were, in the words of historians Samuel Eliot Morison and Henry Steele Commager, "Standard Oil Senators, sugar trust Senators, iron and steel Senators and railroad Senators, men known for their business affiliations rather than for their states." The problem no longer lay with grafters like the Tweed Machine or the Whiskey Ring; lawmaking had been institutionally captured at its source, crippling the constitutional balances set up by the framers.[1]

After Congress authorized bailing out the banks with no accountability and no attention to the too-big-to-fail syndrome that caused the crisis in the first place, it became commonplace for people to say that Wall Street had captured Congress, just as we saw in the 1890s. Even one of the Senate's own members, Dick Durbin of Illinois, went so far as to say that the banks, "frankly, own the place."[2] Then came the Supreme Court's *Citizens United* decision, which showed beyond a reasonable doubt that all three branches of the government had been captured by corporate interests.

It would be easy, under the circumstances, to declare the situation hopeless and retreat into apathy. But this is not a counsel of despair. Man-made problems must yield to man-made solutions. The place to start is the flow of money going into elections.

We can no longer afford to nibble around the edges with another McCain-Feingold act to limit contributions or close loopholes or make other marginal changes that could easily be bypassed. The only rational response after decades of ever-more arcane laws and regulations, and ever-more creative evasions, is to scrap the whole system and start from square one. Get money out of elections—get *all* private money out of our public elections. Federally funded campaigns will undoubtedly create new problems, but can they be remotely as bad as the auctioning of candidates that occurs today? George Will has claimed that the amount of personal and corporate money that flows into U.S. elections is relatively insignificant compared to the national economy; if that is the case, the public can finance a much smaller sum of money to ensure that bribery and extortion do not corrupt the democratic process.

With a small, guaranteed sum to campaign with during a limited campaigning season (perhaps Labor Day until the election, which is generous compared to election campaigns in the United Kingdom, which last less than a month, or Australia, where they last about six weeks) against an opponent who would get the same amount, but no more, we could call an end to the endless campaign season (which in the House begins the day a new member is sworn in) and incumbents could at last spend time governing rather than going to fund-raisers and dialing for dollars outside their congressional offices. The public funding would be a cost-effective investment in the long run. Let us bear in mind that a few hundred thousand dollars in bundled contributions led to a $550 million loss to taxpayers in the Solyndra case; a few million dollars in Halliburton contributions led to billions in waste, fraud, and abuse in Iraq; and a few tens of millions in Wall Street contributions helped cause the loss of trillions to the economy. A politician is a hog that is grateful to whoever is rattling the stick inside the swill bucket. It

is time to take that swill bucket away from corporations and plutocrats.

In lieu of expensive paid advertising, the law should oblige television broadcasters to offer a reasonable but limited amount of free
political advertising during the statutory campaign period. The
broadcasters' permission from the Federal Communications Commission to use publicly owned airwaves gives them a virtual license
to print money—should they not give something back to the public
for that lucrative privilege? I doubt the general public would miss
the blizzard of paid political spots, nor would people regret not receiving robo-calls on the eve of an election. If corporations were to
try to evade the contribution ban by running their own "independent" issue ads on television, there would be no need to litigate the
free speech issues involved. One could require the broadcasters, if
they chose to run such ads, to provide time to a significant opposing viewpoint, given that the corporate ads would be political advocacy touching on the public interest. In the waning days of cigarette
advertising on TV, the tobacco companies faced no outright advertising prohibition; rather, for every block of time they bought, tobacco opponents were permitted time to air a public service
announcement opposing smoking. The antismoking spots were so
devastating that, in the end, the tobacco companies asked the FCC
to take all cigarette ads off the air. If the oil and gas industry wants
to extol "drill, baby, drill" in an issue ad, and believes its cause is
self-evident, it should have no objection to the TV audience's view-
ing a public service announcement about the effects of fracking on
groundwater.

Public financing of elections would not be instituted in order to
maintain the existing parties' duopoly of privilege. Uniform state
requirements would permit third-party or independent candidates
the same rights to ballot access and public financing as would ac-

crue to Democrats or Republicans. Petition requirements could be set high enough to eliminate nuisance candidates but not so high as to prevent legitimate alternatives to the two parties from participating. Open, nonpartisan primaries with the top two finishers contesting the general election could help prevent the current spectacle of hyperpartisan primaries whose winners represent the most extreme faction of the party base.

It would also help solve our present democracy deficit if we joined most of the developed world and had our congressional districts drawn by nonpartisan commissions to represent recognizable geographic areas. The current system of gerrymandering by state legislatures is a corrupt disgrace and would be instantly recognizable to a visitor from the eighteenth century as identical to the system of rotten boroughs in oligarchical Whig England. Adopting rational districts would limit the electoral appeal of extremists, members of family dynasties, and political deadwood in general.

✪

There are other electoral and process reforms that could be instituted, but these are more than enough to begin. Many people would no doubt find utopian, if not otherworldly, what I have just advocated; K Street and the party operatives would certainly be horrified even at the thought of adopting them. But the inescapable point is that without these reforms, or reforms that are substantially similar, all the good-government legislative ideas that anyone has ever had are impossible to enact—the current status quo is wired and locked in to prevent that from happening. It is a telling commentary on what Americans really think about their so-called democracy that changing such a relatively simple and straightforward thing as the financing mechanism for elections is perceived as an unachievable fantasy. Opponents of these ideas must subconsciously believe the Soviet Union of the 1980s was more amenable to reform from below than is the United States of the present day.

On the day when the first Congress meets that is beholden to the public at large rather than to big contributors, its order of business will naturally include changing the tax code, cleaning up Wall Street, and winding down the wars that are impoverishing us financially and morally. But there are other barnacles encrusting the ship of state that need attention.

Antitrust statutes have barely been enforced for thirty years. This circumstance is one of the factors involved in Big Pharma's ability to jack up health-care costs to levels far above those in other developed countries. The government has long banned the reimportation of U.S.-manufactured drugs from foreign countries on the grounds that it is difficult for the Food and Drug Administration to assure the safety of drugs that may have been repackaged, adulterated, or counterfeited. Yet millions of Americans, particularly the elderly, take their chances anyway, ordering medicines from foreign-based Internet pharmacies. Why? Among other reasons, because the Medicare Prescription Drug Act of 2003 prevents the Department of Health and Human Services from negotiating prices for drugs purchased by Medicare beneficiaries. Under this law, Big Pharma gets to sell any particular medicine at full retail price, even if the insurance plan is responsible for millions of orders of it. That is why people may pay from 20 percent, all the way up to 80 percent, less by ordering drugs from abroad. It is also why the ten-year net cost of this law is $550 billion.

The statutory ban on price negotiation with the government amounts to a conspiracy in restraint of trade—as is "pay for delay," whereby pharmaceutical companies pay their competitors not to bring comparable generic drugs to the market. So is the big corporations' "evergreening" of their pharmaceutical patents to artificially extend patent protection: This entails making minor changes to the formula of a prescription drug so that it qualifies as a "new" product subject to patent. Big Pharma will inevitably wail that it needs outsized profits so that it can reinvest that money in the research and development of lifesaving drugs. But Big Pharma spends less on R&D than on the annoying and expensive marketing campaigns for the treatment of questionable medical conditions such as Restless Leg Syndrome, Low T, or ED.

Other than through direct political contributions to candidates, one of the most effective instruments by which corporate America and the plutocratic class maintain disproportionate influence over civic life is the tax-exempt foundation. It is no coincidence that as soon as the income tax came into force in 1913, the Rockefellers, Carnegies, and other tycoons established tax-exempt foundations, ostensibly for charitable and educational purposes. While the executors of such foundations have always stressed their public purpose and burnished their philanthropic images, at their inception the foundations were a tax dodge. Their objective was to create an inextinguishable inheritance that the American Founders abhorred as the basis of the British oligarchy's control over almost all the wealth of Britain.

The reductio ad absurdum of the foundation principle is an outfit like the Heritage Foundation or Grover Norquist's Americans for Tax Reform. The billionaires who make donations to these organizations are engaging in no recognizable form of charity or philanthropy; they are involved in a form of express political advocacy that happens to be tax-exempt. The same applies to defense contractors' contributions to so-called national defense think tanks: It is just a tax-exempt form of advertising or political advocacy. Even much of the charitable support that Goldman Sachs and other corporations give to various projects is in reality an advertising expenditure or a business development investment designed to co-opt, or at least neutralize, any competing centers of influence before they can emerge. And for that they get a tax deduction as a charitable contribution and a bronze plaque thanking them for being such good corporate citizens.

It is time to scrutinize the entire nonprofit sector, particularly the charitable foundations, to see if they meet the letter and spirit of their authorizing statutes. According to the Congressional Research Service, charitable organizations alone had $1.4 trillion in revenue and $2.6 trillion in assets in 2009—a significant percentage of national income to be exempted from taxation.[3] Those that are covert lobbying arms of profit-making contributors should either be obliged to reorganize as nonexempt political advocacy organizations or dissolve. And charitable or otherwise nonprofit organizations should no longer be allowed to compensate their executives at almost the Wall Street level. Does it make sense that an organization should not pay taxes if it can funnel $5.1 million a year into the pocket of its CEO?[4]

Government process reforms to clean up corruption, improve citizen representation, and tame corporate overreach are only first steps, and over time they will become diluted and lose force and effect if the public itself does not perform the hard work of being critically informed and thinking citizens. During the decades since World War II, all manner of illusions and misconceptions have been planted in the national consciousness, and politicians have reinforced them by pandering to the people's flattering self-image of superiority over the rest of the world. According to this narrative, you can cut taxes and increase spending, because tax cuts pay for themselves; we can triumph militarily everywhere if only we have the will to win; and it is solely our superior virtue that could ever make us disliked abroad.

The people of this country must make an effort to clean out their cultural baggage of these and other fondly held illusions: illusions that make it easier for ambitious and manipulative politicians to bamboozle them and build bureaucratic empires that only sap the country's true potential. The foremost of these illusions is the complex of myths that goes by the name American Exceptionalism. No great power or empire is immune to contracting the disease of hubris that gives it an overweening sense of invincibility. Each one of those powers deemed itself as somehow special, uniquely talented, and self-evidently virtuous, and whose founding was inspired by a God who would forever ensure victory on the field of battle. I know of no scientific law or historical precedent that suggests such an immunity for any nation-state. As J. William Fulbright wrote in his book *The Arrogance of Power*:

> The causes of the malady are not entirely clear but its recurrence is one of the uniformities of history: power tends to confuse itself with virtue and a great nation is peculiarly susceptible to the idea that its power is a sign of God's favor, conferring upon it a special responsibility for other nations—to make them richer and happier and wiser, to remake them, that is, in its own shining image.

During my lifetime, one of the most harmful consequences of American Exceptionalism has been the myth of World War II. Americans still lap up the Tom Brokaw fable that Americans somehow won that war single-handedly and as a result of their uniquely virtuous characters. Few Americans know, or care, that Americans suffered less than 1 percent of the global casualties of that war, or that close to 90 percent of all German casualties were sustained fighting the Soviet Union. This is not to say the U.S. contribution was insignificant—it was probably decisive—but it amounted to placing our thumb on the scale rather late in a titanic global struggle. And its principal element was the intelligent exploitation of America's then unparalleled industrial base: The fact that so many Russian boys rode to their deaths in combat in lend-lease trucks from the United States meant that far fewer American boys had to do the same.

That imagined act of winning World War II single-handedly gave us leave to intervene militarily in other countries whenever and wherever we liked, subvert governments we disapproved of, and carry on costly international crusades for the next sixty-five years. But how did our supposed martial virtuosity work out in practice? Was Korea a smashing, unambiguous military triumph? Was Vietnam? Or the 1982 intervention in Lebanon? How about Iraq or Afghanistan, both of which bedevil us still? At least we can notch Panama and Grenada into our rifle butts!

The United States forgot—if it ever knew—the supreme virtue of an enlightened realpolitik, which is to keep one's powder dry, intervene militarily as a last resort (rather than a first), and maintain industrial and fiscal strength at home. Those measures are the surest way of keeping power over the long run. The commentariat, mostly Republicans but also many Democrats, will ritualistically denounce this prescription as simultaneously an ostrichlike ignorance of "threats," based on a naïvely idealistic underestimating of just how dangerous the world is, and a hard-hearted betrayal of "who we are as a nation," given our unbroken record of allegedly altruistic service to mankind. If the reader thinks it takes some effort to be naïvely gullible and narrowly selfish at once, that is because the self-styled internationalists who dominate both parties grasp at any arguments, however contradictory, to rationalize a policy giving them financial and psychic rewards, even as they drive the rest of the country toward bankruptcy. It is long past time for average Americans to switch off *Entertainment Tonight* and become well-informed citizens on foreign and national security policy issues. The professional chicken hawks, whether they are neoconservative empire builders or Democrats desperately trying not to sound weak on defense, trade in myth and mystification that require an apathetic or befuddled audience. If you want politicians to treat you as a citizen rather than as a subject, don't give them reasons to regard you with contempt.

Once we cease squandering trillions on a dead-end military adventurism that creates more enemies than it kills, we will have the resources and the policy focus to concentrate on rejoining the top tier of industrialized nations in public infrastructure, education, and health. The American Society of Civil Engineers (ASCE) estimates that repairing America's surface transportation infrastructure would require an investment of $1.7 trillion by 2020.[5] That's a lot of money; why should we spend enormous sums like that, and where will the money come from? Coincidentally, ASCE's estimate exactly matches what DOD has spent on only the direct cost of its overseas interventions since 2001, including debt service. And ASCE says that our current failing infrastructure raises annual national economic costs, due to increased vehicle operating expenses and travel delays, by $129 billion. That is roughly the average of what the government has spent annually over the last several years on our wars abroad.

There are countless DOD boondoggles beyond the war itself that if ceased could provide potential resources. Does anyone think we are going to improve public schools to the level of those in Finland by laying off teachers and going to four-day weeks? Would investing $35 billion in training teachers and paying them more be at least a start? That is the amount we spent to close unneeded military bases in the past half decade. Base closure is one of those ideas that has great appeal to people who style themselves fiscal conservatives or smart hawks. In theory, the idea is unimpeachable: Why hang on to expensive facilities you don't need? This is why: The Pentagon will use it as an excuse to fold as much cost into the process as possible and gold-plate its remaining bases. First, the base-closing criteria are flawed: While allegedly grounded in the military value of the installation, in practice the process often amounts to closing bases in cold climates in order to shift those functions to existing bases in more southerly climes, where golf can be played all year. The receiving bases generally bulk up with the addition of expensive facilities that have little connection to military readiness: the ubiquitous golf course;* upgraded commissaries for cut-price shopping (an unnecessary facility in all but remote or overseas places; most populated areas near bases have a Sam's Club or Costco just as cheap when the commissary's subsidy is figured into the cost); and new hospital facilities, when the majority of recipients of the military's free health care are retirees, not soldiers or their dependents. The cost-estimating models the military uses overestimate savings from closing a base and underestimate the cost entailed by closing it. Congress exercises next to no scrutiny of the base-closing budget once it approves the list of bases to be closed. As fiscal pressures finally necessitate military downsizing in the next few years, it is a safe bet that the Pentagon will propose another round of base closures that would vitiate much of the savings that are supposed to come from the downsizing. Close excess bases by all means, but base closing cannot be done the way the

---

* Andrews Air Force Base's Web site reads: "Andrews boasts three 18-hole championship courses that are created from an extraordinary design and provides an enjoyable challenge for golfers at all skill levels."

Pentagon set it up to be done in 2005, when the whole process cost taxpayers $35 billion.

There are other aspects of our national security leviathan that need to be scrubbed, if not completely rethought. It is the peculiar conceit of the people who presume to rule us in our name that the American people cannot afford to run *themselves*, but that we can somehow afford to run the rest of the world. The only legitimate expenditures in the foreign affairs budget are the following: sufficient funds to conduct ordinary diplomatic and consular operations (but please, no more Baghdad embassies or similar billion-dollar sinkholes); a revolving fund to pay for disaster and humanitarian relief contingencies; funding for the monitoring and eradication of communicable diseases abroad (which has a clear benefit to everyone in an age of air travel, including the U.S. population); monitoring of nuclear proliferation; and support for international organizations, if they provide a worthwhile function and our contribution is cheaper than if we did it ourselves. That's it.

What we do not need, except under the most extraordinary circumstances, is so-called security assistance, meaning bribes to pliable dictators or otherwise corrupt countries' officials wishing to ingratiate themselves to us, all underwritten by the U.S. taxpayer. Dumping free or subsidized weapons on every area of potential conflict around the globe has had a nasty habit of boomeranging, as regimes change or weapons leak into the wrong hands (and they were probably never in the right hands to begin with). Arming the shah of Iran to the teeth did not work out very well, nor did supplying cluster bombs to Saddam Hussein in the 1980s. Arming the Afghan mujahedin during that same decade, and particularly the manner in which we did it (using Saudi and Pakistani intelligence agencies as cutouts) may have been the single most consequential policy blunder since Vietnam. And the Made in USA label probably does not make a good impression on the local population when it is printed on the canister of a particularly potent teargas employed in Cairo's Tahrir Square, or on a cattle prod used in a Moroccan interrogation cell.

By the same token, we do not need to provide the kind of development assistance that do-gooders claim is virtuous but ends up granting a free lunch to Halliburton, Bechtel, Parsons, and other vultures. This assistance also showers payola on the kleptocrats running the countries involved. We have seen too many abandoned steel mills in the Congo, ice cream plants in Egypt, and white-elephant power plants in India (the last with loans guaranteed by the taxpayer and built by Enron, GE, and Bechtel). Other cultures stubbornly remain what they are, and no amount of missionary zeal, do-gooding, or bribery is likely to change that. This futile activity has been going on for decades: The United States spent then astronomical sums to irrigate the Helmand Valley and create the American-style town of Lashkar Gah in 1950s' Afghanistan. The development lobby, the security assistance lobby, and the corporations behind them are politically strong and will make superficially plausible national interest arguments to keep the money flowing. They will always argue that such spending is such a tiny percentage of the federal budget, or of U.S. GDP, that it is not worth cutting it. It is true that it is a relatively small amount of money in those terms, but would not $15 billion a year at least help construct water-filtration plants, smart electric grids, or advanced fuel-efficient transportation in this country—especially as the money would otherwise largely be wasted or spent in ways we might ultimately regret?

The key factor is that there is spending and there is spending. A carpenter who spends all he can spare to buy an excellent set of tools is investing; if he spends the same amount on a down payment for a luxury car, he is squandering. "Realistic" politicians and their media echo chamber are constantly telling us we can't afford to retire, drive on decent roads, or even live as long as people in the rest of the developed world. They are usually the same people who insist that to remain the leader of the free world, we must keep pouring money down rat holes. With a $15 trillion debt, a global empire is a luxury we can no more afford than a paycheck-to-paycheck laborer can afford a Bentley.

Adjusted for inflation, the United States during the Great Depression had less than one tenth of our country's current gross domestic product. Unemployment then was more than double ours now. There were national security threats on the horizon. The hit song of 1932 was "Brother, Can You Spare a Dime?" Yet that generation constructed the Hoover Dam, the Grand Coulee Dam, the Tennessee Valley Authority, and the Golden Gate Bridge. It built or refurbished sewer and water systems and other public infrastructure, brought electricity to rural America, established places of recreation, from city parks to national parks, so that citizens could glimpse a more spacious and abundant life, and forged an industrial machine that was the wonder and envy of the world. A few years later that economic dynamo could build a Liberty ship a day and nearly a hundred thousand military aircraft a year. A couple of years after that the United States flooded the world with its new industrial goods, sparking a rising and optimistic middle-class economy—not only in America but in other parts of the globe.

With our vastly greater material base, it would seem we could achieve a national reconstruction every bit as impressive as that achieved between 1933 and 1945. But what of the human factors? Despite everything I have said about the current sad state of government, I know from three decades' personal experience that there are countless honest, dedicated, and patriotic Americans working in all three branches and at all levels of government. They want to do a good job but are blocked, hamstrung, and demoralized by what can only be described as a corrupt and ossified political system.

Although I have severely criticized Congress as a dysfunctional institution, it will not repair itself if bright, idealistic young people stay away from it. I left it because I was old, worn out, and conscious of the fact that there is a point in life when it is simply time to go. But having had a minor hand in halting some extravagant government programs like the B-2 and a few others, I believe my time on Capitol Hill was well spent. If we are to mend our broken government, perhaps the cream of our universities' graduating classes might think twice about Wall Street or corporate law, and try public service instead.

Beyond government, among the American people at large, there is reason for tentative optimism. Despite the politicians' attempts at infecting them with the cynical belief that they won't get their Social Security, and that politics and governance are just a con game for fat cats, the generation born after about 1982 may yet give us cause for hope. Authors William Strauss and Neil Howe called this generation the Millennials in a book of the same name.[6] As with any generalization about complex social phenomena, one can criticize some of their more breathless deductions about the generation that began to reach adulthood during the decade of the 2000s. But I conclude from my own observation that the Millennials are generally optimistic and socially conscious while at the same time they shun the baby boomers' signature traits of self-righteous cant and narcissistic sense of entitlement. It is the baby boomers right now for the most part who are running the show. Over the next decade the boomers' grip on power will begin to loosen, and along with that welcome development, their tiresome and sterile obsessions about the culture wars of the 1960s may at last reside in the dustbin of history. It is just possible that the rising generation of adults will approach the problems they face not with cookie-cutter formulas based on what is politically correct, scripturally correct, or what conforms to the dogma of some long-dead crackpot "thinker," but on what works.

If our grandparents and great-grandparents operating with the slenderest resources could accomplish the transformation of the worst economic circumstances in American history into the heyday of the more abundant life, so can the present generation work its way out of our current troubles. Distraction, mystification, fearmongering, and the stoking of hatred are the tools that keep the American people in an apathetic and childish state. Creative and constructive work is always harder than demagoguery or fearmongering; we have had too little of the former and too much of the latter during recent decades. At many other times Americans have overcome comparable or greater difficulties, even if the specific issues they confronted were different from our current ones. On December 1, 1862, as insurrectionist armies were encamped barely fifty miles from the national capital, Abraham Lincoln had this to say to a restive Congress:

> The dogmas of the quiet past are inadequate to the stormy present. The occasion is piled high with difficulty, and we must rise with the occasion. As our case is new, so we must think anew and act anew.

ACKNOWLEDGMENTS

I owe a debt of gratitude to Franklin C. "Chuck" Spinney for laboring through a rough draft of this work and making valuable suggestions to improve it. He detected errors of fact and interpretation that only a seasoned scholar of the national security establishment such as Chuck could have found. He also provided the unwavering encouragement necessary for me to carry through with writing this book. Eric Lofgren provided a millennial's fresh perspective on the dreary political battles we baby boomers have been fighting for so many decades. Most of all, I would like to acknowledge the unstinting loyalty and boundless patience of my wife, Alisa, for enduring the Sturm und Drang of the writing process.

NOTES

INTRODUCTION

1. "A Harsh Case Against Obama and His Opponents," *The Atlantic*, September 3, 2011; www.theatlantic.com/politics/archive/2011/09/a-harsh-case-against-obama-and-his-opponents/244512/.
2. "Congress' Approval Problem in One Chart," *Washington Post*, November 15, 2011; www.washingtonpost.com/blogs/the-fix/post/congress-approval-problem-in-one-chart/2011/11/15/gIQAkHmtON_blog.html#excerpt.

CHAPTER 1   THE PARTY OF LINCOLN, THE PARTY OF JEFFERSON

1. Bill Moyers, "Our Politicians Are Money Launderers in the Trafficking of Power and Policy," Thruthout.com, November 3, 2011; www.truth-out.org/how-did-happen/1320278111.
2. "A Long, Steep Drop for Americans' Standard of Living," *Christian Science Monitor*, October 19, 2011; www.csmonitor.com/Business/2011/1019/A-long-steep-drop-for-Americans-standard-of-living.
3. "Social Justice in the OECD—How Do the Member States Compare?" Bertelsmann Foundation; www.sgi-network.org/pdf/SGI11_Social_Justice_OECD.pdf.
4. "Trends in the Distribution of Household Income Between 1979 and 2007," Congressional Budget Office, October 2011; www.cbo.gov/doc.cfm?index=12485.
5. http://econ161.berkeley.edu/economists/keynes.html.

CHAPTER 2   TACTICS: WAR MINUS THE SHOOTING

1. "If Obama Likes Lincoln So Much, He Should Start Acting Like Him," *The New Republic*, July 30, 2011; www.tnr.com/article/john-judis/92958/obama-lincoln-debt-ceiling.
2. "Scalia: Our Political System Is 'Designed for' Gridlock," *The Atlantic*, October 6, 2011; www.theatlantic.com/national/archive/2011/10/scalia-our-political-system-is-designed-for-gridlock/246257/.
3. "Economic Experts Gather in DC to Explain Why Politics Has Doomed Us,"

Talkingpointsmemo.com, December 9, 2011; http://tpmdc.talkingpoints memo.com/2011/12/economic-experts-gather-in-dc-to-explain-why-politics-has-doomed-us.php.

CHAPTER 3   ALL WRAPPED UP IN THE CONSTITUTION

1. "Ashcroft Defends Proposal to Toss Gun Records," Associated Press, July 25, 2002; www.foxnews.com/story/0,2933,58728,00.html.
2. "At Hearing About ATF Program, Issa Mutes Witness for Promoting Gun Law Reforms," *The Hill*, June 15, 2011; http://thehill.com/blogs/blog-briefing-room/news/166715-at-hearing-about-atf-program-issa-mutes-witness-for-promoting-gun-law-reforms.
3. "Doctors Sue Rick Scott over Law Banning Them from Asking Patients About Guns," *Orlando Sentinel*, June 6, 2011; http://articles.orlandosentinel.com/2011-06-06/health/os-docs-sue-rick-scott-20110606_1_national-gun-control-group-gun-ownership-rick-scott.

CHAPTER 4   A DEVIL'S DICTIONARY

1. "Iraq 'Behind US Anthrax Outbreaks,'" *The Observer* (UK), October 14, 2001; www.guardian.co.uk/world/2001/oct/14/terrorism.afghanistan6.
2. www.informationclearinghouse.info/article4443.htm.

CHAPTER 5   TAXES AND THE RICH

1. "House Protects Pizza as a Vegetable," Reuters, November 18, 2011; www.reuters.com/article/2011/11/18/us-usa-lunch-idUSTRE7AH00020111118.
2. "Top 3 Domestic Food Manufacturers," *Corporations and Health*; www.corporationsandhealth.org/resources/food-industry.
3. "ConAgra," Sourcewatch.com; www.sourcewatch.org/index.php?title=Con Agra.
4. "In China, Human Costs Are Built Into an iPad," *New York Times*, January 25, 2012; www.nytimes.com/2012/01/26/business/ieconomy-apples-ipad-and-the-human-costs-for-workers-in-china.html?pagewanted=all.
5. "U.S. Small Business Sector One of the Smallest Amongst Comparable Countries," Center for Economic and Policy Research, August 3, 2009; www.cepr.net/index.php/press-releases/press-releases/us-small-business-sector-among-the-smallest-in-the-world/.
6. "GOP: Python Ban Squeezes Economy," *Politico*, September 14, 2011; http://dyn.politico.com/printstory.cfm?uuid=04F59EC8-DDB8-49C8-93A1-8F09E3F40EC5; "Broken Government: How the Administrative State Has Broken President Obama's Promise of Regulatory Reform," Committee on Oversight and Government Reform, September 14, 2011; http://oversight.house.gov/images/stories/Reports/9.13.11_Broken_Government_Report.pdf.
7. "The Numbers: How Do U.S. Taxes Compare Internationally?" Tax Policy

Center; www.taxpolicycenter.org/briefing-book/background/numbers/inter
national.cfm.

8. "Rep. Bachus Tells Local Paper That Washington Should 'Serve' Banks," *The Hill*, December 13, 2010; http://thehill.com/blogs/on-the-money/banking-financial-institutions/133379-bachus-tells-local-paper-that-washington-should-qserveq-banks.

9. "Inside the Cain Tax Plan," *New York Times*, October 11, 2011; http://econo mix.blogs.nytimes.com/2011/10/11/inside-the-cain-tax-plan/.

10. Howard Gleckman, "Cain's 9-9-9 Plan Would Cut Taxes for the Rich, Raise Taxes for Almost Everyone Else," Tax Policy Center, October 18, 2011; http://taxvox.taxpolicycenter.org/2011/10/18/cain%E2%80%99s-9-9-9-plan-would-cut-taxes-for-the-rich-raise-taxes-for-almost-everyone-else/.

11. "Cain Adviser Says 9-9-9 Plan Didn't Take an Economist to Create," *Bloomberg Businessweek*, October 14, 2011; www.businessweek.com/news/2011-10-14/cain-adviser-says-9-9-9-plan-didn-t-take-an-economist-to-create .html; http://en.wikipedia.org/wiki/Gates_Mills,_Ohio.

12. "Gingrich's Tax Plan: Big Tax Cuts, Big Deficits," Tax Policy Center, December 12, 2011; http://taxvox.taxpolicycenter.org/2011/12/12/gingrich%e2% 80%99s-tax-plan-big-tax-cuts-big-deficits/.

13. "The Romney Tax Plan," Tax Policy Center, January 5, 2012; http://taxpolicy center.org/taxtopics/upload/description-Romney-plan.pdf.

14. "Primary Numbers: The GOP Candidates and the National Debt," A Committee for a Responsible Federal Budget Project; http://crfb.org/sites/default/ files/primary_numbers.pdf.

15. "GOP Walks Away from Payroll Tax Debacle Bruised," National Public Radio, December 24, 2011; www.npr.org/2011/12/24/144219480/gop-walks-away-from-payroll-tax-debacle-bruised.

CHAPTER 6 WORSHIPPING AT THE ALTAR OF MARS

1. "Republican Group Under Fire for Email Featuring Obama Shot in Head," ABC News, October 31, 2011; http://abcnews.go.com/blogs/politics/2011/10/ republican-group-under-fire-for-email-featuring-obama-shot-in-head/.

2. "Government Pays More in Contracts, Study Finds," *New York Times*, September 12, 2011; www.nytimes.com/2011/09/13/us/13contractor.html?_r=2.

3. "U.S. Defense on the Defensive," *Washington Post*, November 6, 2011; www .washingtonpost.com/opinions/defense-on-the-rocks/2011/11/04/gIQA KQDctM_story.html.

4. "Study: Youngstown Has Highest Poverty Rate in U.S.," WKBN News, November 3, 2011; www.wkbn.com/content/news/local/story/Study-Youngs town-Has-Highest-Poverty-Rate-in-U-S/qljniy5c9keJpSz3p2ArmA.cspx.

5. "Toledo Area Poverty Rates Named Worst in the Nation," Northwestohio .com, November 4, 2011; www.northwestohio.com/news/story.aspx?id= 682599.

6. "More Half-Measures from Obama Administration on Iran," *Washington Post*, November 22, 2011; www.washingtonpost.com/opinions/more-half-measures-from-obama-administration-on-iran/2011/11/22/gIQADX xLmN_story.html.

7. "Al-Qaeda Targets Dwindle as Group Shrinks," *Washington Post*, November 22, 2011; www.washingtonpost.com/world/national-security/al-qaeda-targets-dwindle-as-group-shrinks/2011/11/22/gIQAbXJNmN_story.html.

CHAPTER 7 MEDIA COMPLICITY

1. "The Centrist Cop-Out," *New York Times*, July 28, 2011; www.nytimes .com/2011/07/29/opinion/krugman-the-centrist-cop-out.html?_r=3&hp.

2. "Should the Times Be a Truth Vigilante?," *New York Times*, January 12, 2012; http://publiceditor.blogs.nytimes.com/2012/01/12/should-the-times-be-a-truth-vigilante/.

3. "World Press Freedom Index 2011–2012," *Reporters without Borders*, January 25, 2012; http://en.rsf.org/IMG/CLASSEMENT_2012/C_GENERAL_ANG.pdf.

4. "Tavis Smiley on Morning Joe: Bush 'Lied' Us into Iraq," TheRawStory.com, September 12, 2011; www.rawstory.com/rawreplay/2011/09/tavis-smiley-on-morning-joe-bush-lied-us-into-iraq/.

5. "Radical Son: Bush May Not Have Read Dostoyevsky—But His Speechwriters Have," YuricaReport.com, February 28, 2005;_www.yuricareport.com/BushSecondTerm/MoreOnBushSecondInaugural.html.

6. "Iran May Have Sent Libya Shells for Chemical Weapons," *Washington Post*, November 20, 2011; www.washingtonpost.com/world/national-security/iran-may-have-sent-libya-shells-for-chemical-weapons/2011/11/18/gIQA 7RPifN_story.html.

7. "U.S. Officials: Iran Is Stepping Up Lethal Aid to Syria," *Washington Post*, March 3, 2012; www.washingtonpost.com/world/national-security/us-officials-iran-is-stepping-up-lethal-aid-to-syria/2012/03/02/gIQA GR9XpR_story.html?hpid=z1.

CHAPTER 8 GIVE ME THAT OLD-TIME RELIGION

1. "Rep. Walsh Lauded by Group for Being Pro-Family, Though Accused of Owing Child Support," *Chicago Sun-Times*, November 6, 2011; www.sun times.com/news/politics/8598963-418/rep-walsh-lauded-by-group-for-being-pro-family-though-accused-of-owing-child-support.html.

2. "God Is Pro-war," WND.com, January 31, 2004; www.wnd.com/news/arti cle.asp?ARTICLE_ID=36859.

3. "'Road Map Is a Life Saver for Us,' PM Abbas Tells Hamas," *Haaretz*, June 24, 2003; www.haaretz.com/print-edition/news/road-map-is-a-life-saver-for-us-pm-abbas-tells-hamas-1.92200.

4. "Michele Bachmann: The First 2012er to Get Koch Cash," *Mother Jones*, July

15, 2011; http://motherjones.com/mojo/2011/07/michele-Bachmann-koch-brothers-201.

5. "Being a Christian Is No Excuse for Being Stupid," RightWingWatch.org, September 18, 2006; www.rightwingwatch.org/2006/09/being_a_christian_is_no_excuse_for_being_stupid.html.

6. "Tea Party's Dick Armey: A GOP Majority Would Take Up Abortion Fight," *The Christian Science Monitor*, September 13, 2010; www.csmonitor.com/USA/Politics/monitor_breakfast/2010/0913/Tea-party-s-Dick-Armey-A-GOP-majority-would-take-up-abortion-fight.

7. "Crashing the Tea Party," *New York Times*, August 17, 2011; http://mobile.nytimes.com/article?a=829691&single=1&f=126.

8. "Tea Party Supporters Overlap Republican Base," Gallup, July 2, 2010; www.gallup.com/poll/141098/Tea-Party-Supporters-Overlap-Republican-Base.aspx?version=print.

9. "Religion and the Tea Party in the 2010 Election," Public Religion Research Institute, October 2010; http://publicreligion.org/site/wp-content/uploads/2010/05/Religion-and-the-Tea-Party-in-the-2010-Election-American-Values-Survey.pdf.

10. "Death Panels Begin as Reform Takes Shape," www.teaparty.org/article.php?id=186 (reprinted from *Investor's Business Daily* by the Tea Party).

11. "More Now Disagree with Tea Party—Even in Tea Party Districts," Pew Research Center, November 29, 2011; www.people-press.org/2011/11/29/more-now-disagree-with-tea-party-%E2%80%93-even-in-tea-party-districts/.

12. "Did the American Pope Really Bless Ryan's Budget?" *Time*, May 24, 2011; http://swampland.time.com/2011/05/24/did-the-american-pope-bless-ryans-budget/#ixzz1h1W5m9cI.

13. "Rick Perry's Army of God," *Texas Observer*, August 3, 2011; www.texasobserver.org/cover-story/rick-perrys-army-of-god.

14. "Candidates (Except Romney) Gather in Iowa for Doomiest and Gloomiest Debate of All," TalkingPointsMemo.com, November 19, 2011; http://2012.talkingpointsmemo.com/2011/11/candiates-except-romney-gather-in-iowa-for-doomiest-and-gloomiest-debate-of-all.php?ref=fpnewsfeed_beta.

15. Robert Altemeyer, *The Authoritarians*, 2006; http://members.shaw.ca/jean altemeyer/drbob/TheAuthoritarians.pdf.

CHAPTER 9 NO EGGHEADS WANTED

1. Lionel Trilling, *The Liberal Imagination*, 1950.

2. "Michigan Senate OKs Anti-Bullying Bill Despite Protests," *The Detroit News*, November 3, 2011; www.detnews.com/article/20111103/POLITICS02/111030376/1022/Michigan-Senate-OKs-anti-bullying-bill-despite-protests.

3. "Herman Cain Incorrectly Suggests China Doesn't Have Nuclear Capability," CBS News, November 2, 2011; www.cbsnews.com/8301-503544_162-201

28920-503544/herman-cain-incorrectly-suggests-china-doesnt-have-nuclear-capability/.

4. "Nobody's Gonna Make Herman Cain Talk About Foreign Policy If He Doesn't Want To," *Foreign Policy*, October 11, 2011; http://blog.foreignpolicy.com/posts/2011/10/11/nobodys_gonna_make_herman_cain_talk_about_foreign_policy_if_he_doesnt_want_to.

5. "Rick Perry to Announce Flat Tax as Part of Economic Plan," *Washington Post*, October 19, 2011; www.washingtonpost.com/politics/rick-perry-to-announce-flat-tax-as-part-of-economic-plan/2011/10/19/gIQAuWn1xL_story.html.

6. "Santorum: Parents, Not Obama, Know What Is Best for Their Child's Education," *Des Moines Register*, December 9, 2011; http://caucuses.desmoinesregister.com/2011/12/09/santorum-parents-not-obama-know-what-is-best-for-their-childs-education/.

7. "'The Wedge Document:' 'So What?'" The Discovery Institute (undated); www.discovery.org/scripts/viewDB/filesDB-download.php?id=349.

8. *Conservapedia*, www.conservapedia.com/Main_Page.

9. "Latest German Fad: Leasing Out the Subway," *New York Times*, July 10, 2003; www.nytimes.com/2003/07/10/business/latest-german-fad-leasing-out-the-subway.html?pagewanted=all&src=pm.

10. "Upton Sinclair and the Wonk Gap," *New York Times*, January 18, 2011; http://krugman.blogs.nytimes.com/2011/01/18/upton-sinclair-and-the-wonk-gap/.

11. "Two Contests for the GOP Nomination," *Washington Post*, October 24, 2011; www.washingtonpost.com/blogs/the-insiders/post/two-contests-for-the-gop-nomination/2011/10/20/gIQAPfGEAM_blog.html.

12. "Faith, Certainty and the Presidency of George W. Bush," *New York Times*, October 17, 2004; www.nytimes.com/2004/10/17/magazine/17BUSH.html?_r=3.

CHAPTER 10   A LOW DISHONEST DECADE

1. Testimony of Alan Greenspan before the House Committee on the Budget, March 2, 2001; www.gpo.gov/fdsys/pkg/CHRG-107hhrg70749/pdf/CHRG-107hhrg70749.pdf.

2. Stanley Milgram, *Obedience to Authority: An Experimental View*, 1974.

3. "Tribute to Nuremberg Prosecutor Jackson," speech by Benjamin B. Ferencz; www.roberthjackson.org/the-man/speeches-articles/speeches/speeches-related-to-robert-h-jackson/tribute-to-nuremberg-prosecutor-jackson/

4. Robert H. Jackson, "Summation for the Prosecution," July 26, 1946; http://law2.umkc.edu/faculty/projects/ftrials/nuremberg/Jackson.html.

5. *International Conference on Military Trials*, Department of State publication, 1949; http://en.wikiquote.org/wiki/Robert_H._Jackson.

6. "Share Traders More Reckless Than Psychopaths, Study Shows," *Der Spiegel*, September 26, 2011; www.spiegel.de/international/zeitgeist/0,1518,788462,00.html.

7. "1978 Speech by Gingrich," www.pbs.org/wgbh/pages/frontline/newt/newt 78speech.html.

CHAPTER 11   ARE THE DEMOCRATS ANY BETTER?

1. "Who Wants to Vote for a Multimillionaire?" *Time*, June 7, 2000; www.time .com/time/nation/article/0,8599,46866,00.html.
2. "Rick Scott: Florida's Drug Fraud Enabler?" *Mother Jones*, March 8, 2011; http://motherjones.com/mojo/2011/03/rick-scott-floridas-drug-fraud-enabler.
3. "Pakistan Doubles Its Nuclear Arsenal," *Washington Post*, January 31, 2011; www.washingtonpost.com/wp-dyn/content/article/2011/01/30/AR2011013004682.html.

CHAPTER 12   A WAY OUT?

1. Kevin Phillips, *Wealth and Democracy: A Political History of the American Rich*, 2003.
2. "Dick Durbin: Banks 'Frankly Own the Place,'" HuffingtonPost.com, May 30, 2009.
3. "An Overview of the Nonprofit and Charitable Sector," Congressional Research Service, November 17, 2009; www.fas.org/sgp/crs/misc/R40919.pdf.
4. "Slideshow: Who Are the Highest-Paid Nonprofit Executives?" *Dallas Business Journal*, September 16, 2011; www.bizjournals.com/dallas/blog/2011/09/slideshow-who-are-the-highest-paid.html.
5. "Decaying Infrastructure Costs U.S. Billions Each Year, Report Says," *Washington Post*, July 27, 2011; www.washingtonpost.com/local/decaying-infrastructure-costing-us-billions-report-says/2011/07/27/gIQAAI0zcI_story.html.
6. Neil Howe and William Strauss, *Millennials Rising: The Next Great Generation*, 2000.

INDEX